N.A.P.B.L.
UMPIRE
MANUAL

N.A.P.B.L. UMPIRE MANUAL

UMPIRE DEVELOPMENT PROGRAM

BOOKS

CHICAGO

Major League Baseball Umpire Development Program
P. O. Box A
St. Petersburg, Florida 33731

Some material contained herein has been used
with acknowledgment from the following:

The American League of Professional Baseball Clubs
The National League of Professional Baseball Clubs

Cover photo courtesy of Barbara White.

Tom Lepperd, Editor

Triumph Books
644 South Clark Street
Chicago, Illinois 60605
(312) 939-3330
(312) 663-3557 FAX

CONTENTS

SECTION 1
EQUIPMENT, PLAYERS, AND THE PLAYING FIELD

SECTION 2
LINEUPS AND SUBSTITUTIONS

SECTION 3
APPEALS AND AWARDS

SECTION 4
INTERFERENCE AND OBSTRUCTION

SECTION 5
PROGRESS OF THE GAME

SECTION 6
PITCHING REGULATIONS

SECTION 7
INSTRUCTIONS TO UMPIRES

SECTION 8
MECHANICS FOR THE THREE-UMPIRE SYSTEM

SECTION 9
MECHANICS FOR THE FOUR-UMPIRE SYSTEM

FOREWORD

The integrity of baseball is embodied in the Umpire upon whom the trust is placed to insure the game is played by the rules guaranteeing fairness for those involved. During the course of performing these prescribed duties, the Umpire must at times interpret and clarify rules as they are written. Words can never be written to cover all situations in our great game and therefore incidents may occur which call for the sound and fair judgment of the Umpire. This publication contains interpretations, clarifications, general practices, and rulings endorsed by the National Association of Professional Baseball Leagues and the Umpire Development Program. It is provided as a supplement to the Official Baseball Playing Rules which govern all games in the National Association.

Mike Moore

MIKE MOORE, PRESIDENT
National Association
of Professional Baseball Leagues

CHANGES FROM PREVIOUS EDITION

The following sections of this edition of the *N.A.P.B.L. Umpire Manual* contain changes and revisions from the last edition:

1.6

1.19

Rating Scale

7.29

SECTION 1

EQUIPMENT, PLAYERS, AND THE PLAYING FIELD

1.1 PROTECTIVE HEADGEAR

All players shall wear a double ear-flap helmet while at bat. All runners shall wear protective headgear while on base. (Note: Major League players on a rehab assignment with an N.A. club may wear a single ear-flap helmet while at bat in a Minor League game.)

All bat/ball boys or girls shall wear a protective helmet while performing their duties. This rule is to be strictly enforced by the umpire and all club personnel.

All catchers shall wear a catcher's protective helmet while fielding their position.

1.2 CONDUCT OF PLAYERS DURING PROGRESS OF GAME

During the progress of a game, all players of the club at bat must be on the bench except when they have some duty to perform as coaches, base runners, batter, or on-deck batter. Players of the side at bat will not be permitted to fraternize with players in the bullpen either of their own or of the visiting club, but must come to their own bench even if, in their judgment, they are not likely to bat in the inning. Base runners retired before reaching first base or put out on the bases must return to the bench until the inning is ended.

No one except players in uniform, substitutes in uniform, coaches in uniform, managers, trainers, and bat boys shall occupy a bench during a game.

Only pitchers, catchers, and players serving as catchers should be permitted to stay in the bullpen during the game.

A substitute player who will enter the game at the end of the half inning or a designated hitter who will enter the game as a defensive player will be permitted to warm up in the bullpen.

Players removed from the game (other than by an umpire) may warm up pitchers and may act as base coaches.

1.3 RESTRICTIONS ON PITCHERS WARMING UP

The home club pitcher may not warm up on the mound prior to the start of the game. He may take only his eight preparatory pitches on the mound. This could give the home club pitcher some advantage, and since pre-game practice conditions should be equal for both starting pitchers, both pitchers should warm up where pitchers normally warm up.

Following a rain delay, it is permissible for the pitcher of the defensive team to warm up on the mound. When the side is retired, the opposing pitcher will be granted extra time, if needed, to warm up on the mound. Umpires are to use good common sense in situations of this nature.

If a pitcher changes defensive positions and then returns to the mound during the same inning, he will be allowed the usual eight warm-up pitches.

If a sudden emergency causes a pitcher to be summoned into the game without opportunity to warm up (e.g., game pitcher is injured or ejected), the umpire shall allow the new pitcher as many pitches as the umpire deems necessary.

A pitcher who is already in the game may go back to warm up in the bullpen between innings provided he does not delay the game.

1.4 PLAYERS ON DISABLED LIST

Players on the disabled list are permitted to participate in pre-game activity and may sit in uniform on the bench during a game but may not take part in any activity during the game such as warming up a pitcher, bench jockeying, etc. Disabled players are not allowed to enter the playing surface at any time or for any purpose during the game.

1.5 EJECTIONS AND SUSPENSIONS

When a manager, player, coach, or trainer is ejected from a game, he shall leave the field immediately and take no further part in that game. He shall remain in the clubhouse or change to street clothes and either leave the park or take a seat in the grandstand well removed from the vicinity of his team's bench or bullpen. He may not stand in the runway between the clubhouse and dugout.

Any person ejected from a game shall leave the dugout and shall not stand in the runway. If a person who has been ejected continues to appear in the runway area, umpires should not delay the game by repeatedly insisting that the person leave. In such instances, the offender has seriously violated the rules, and the umpiring crew shall report this fact to the league president.

If a manager, coach, player, or trainer is under suspension, he shall leave the field before the game starts, change to street clothes, and either leave the park or take a seat in the grandstand well removed from the vicinity of his club's bench and bullpen. If under suspension, he may not be in the dugout or press box during a game.

1.6 PLAYER CHARGING THE PITCHER'S MOUND

A batter, runner, or other player charging or pursuing the pitcher will receive an automatic fine (<u>minimum</u> $150 at Class AAA, $100 at Class AA,

$50 at Class A, $25 at Short-Season and Rookie). Additionally, if such player is deemed by the league president to have been an **instigator or combatant** in a confrontation, such automatic fine will be increased to a minimum of $450, $300, $150, and $75, respectively, *and* a minimum three-game suspension will apply. *(See Section 7.29, "On-Field Behavior Policy.")*

A batter, runner, or other player charging or pursuing the pitcher may also be ejected from the game if, in the umpire's judgment, circumstances warrant.

In addition to the above-mentioned penalties, any member of the offensive team who charges the pitcher's mound will be automatically ejected from the game if he reaches the dirt portion of the mound.

1.7 ON-DECK BATTER

The next batter up must be in the on-deck circle, and this is the only player who should be there (i.e., **not more than one player at a time**). This shall be strictly enforced. No other player of the side at bat will be permitted on the field except the batter, base runners, and coaches.

1.8 PINE TAR ON BAT

The bat handle for not more than eighteen inches from its end may be covered or treated with any material or substance to improve the grip. Any such material or substance which extends past the eighteen-inch limitation shall cause the bat to be removed from the game.

NOTE: If the umpire discovers that the bat does not conform to this regulation until a time during or after which the bat has been used in play, it shall not be grounds for declaring the batter out or being ejected from the game.

Official Rule 6.06(d) prohibits the use of "doctored" bats. The use of pine tar in itself shall not be considered doctoring the bat. (See Section 1.20, "Altered or Tampered Bats.")

1.9 BATTER'S POSITION IN BATTER'S BOX

The lines defining the batter's box are considered within the batter's box. When the batter assumes his position in the batter's box, he shall have both feet completely within the batter's box; i.e., no part of either foot may extend beyond the lines defining the box when the batter assumes his position.

If a batter hits a ball (fair, foul, or foul tip) with one or both feet on the ground entirely outside the batter's box, he shall be declared out.

1.10 BATTER STEPPING OUT OF BATTER'S BOX

Once a batter has taken his position in the batter's box, he shall not be permitted to step out of the batter's box in order to use the resin or the pine tar rag unless there is a delay in the game action or, in the judgment of the umpires, weather conditions warrant an exception. This rule is to be strictly enforced.

If after the pitcher starts his windup or comes to a set position with a runner on, he does not go through with his pitch because the batter has stepped out of the box, it shall not be called a balk. Both the pitcher and batter have violated a rule, and the umpire shall call time and both the batter and pitcher start over from "scratch."

If the pitcher delays once the batter is in his box and the umpire feels that the delay is not justified, he may allow the batter to step out of the box momentarily.

1.11 ARGUING BALLS AND STRIKES

Players leaving their position in the field or on base, or managers or coaches leaving the bench or coach's box to argue on balls and strikes will not be permitted. They should be warned if they start for the plate or otherwise leave their position to protest the call. If they continue, they will be ejected from the game.

1.12 CHECKED SWINGS

An appeal may be made when the plate umpire calls a pitch a ball on a checked swing. In such an instance the plate umpire shall make an immediate call but must appeal to the appropriate base umpire if requested by the defensive manager or catcher. The plate umpire may—on his own volition—ask for help from the appropriate base umpire if in doubt on a checked swing.

If the crew is working with three umpires, the plate umpire shall always ask for help from the first base umpire with a right-handed batter at bat and shall ask for help from the third base umpire with a left-handed batter at bat.

In situations when there are two strikes on the batter and the next pitch is *a passed ball or wild pitch (or other pitch which eludes the catcher)* on which there is a check swing, the proper procedure is for the plate umpire to ask the base umpire for help **IMMEDIATELY** (while the catcher is retrieving the ball), *without waiting for an appeal request from the defense*. This way, both the defense and offense are quickly advised as to what the final call will be.

Managers, coaches, or players may not argue the call (or the appealed decision) on a checked swing. If a manager, coach, or player leaves his position to argue with any umpire concerning the decision on a checked swing, he shall be warned that this is not permitted. If he persists in arguing, the offender shall be removed from the game, as he is now arguing over a called ball or strike.

All decisions on checked swings shall be called **loudly and clearly** by the plate umpire. If the pitch is a ball and the batter does not swing at the pitch, the mechanic to be used by the plate umpire is: "Ball; no, he didn't go." If the pitch is a ball but the batter commits on the check swing, the mechanic to be used is: "Yes he went," while pointing directly at the batter and then coming up with the strike motion.

The umpire's decision on a check swing shall be based entirely on his judgment as to whether or not the batter struck at the pitch.

Baserunners and umpires must be alert to the possibility that the base umpire—on a checked swing appeal from the plate umpire—may reverse the call of a ball to the call of a strike, in which event the runner is in jeopardy of being put out by the catcher's throw. Also, the catcher and umpire must be alert in base-stealing situations if a ball call is reversed to a strike by the base umpire upon appeal from the plate umpire. For example, consider the following play:

Play: Runner on first base, 3-1 count on the batter. Runner is stealing, and there is a check swing on the pitch. Plate umpire calls, "Ball; no, he didn't go." Catcher throws the ball to second base anyway, resulting in a play at second where the runner is tagged before reaching second base.

Ruling: The base umpire should watch the play closely but make no call on the play because when the tag play occurs at second base it actually *is* ball four—and will continue to be—until an appeal is made, and even then it will remain ball four unless the check swing is reversed. Therefore, after the play at second base is completed the base umpire should merely announce, "That's ball four" in order to avoid any confusion on the part of the players. If the defensive manager or catcher requests an appeal on the check swing, the plate umpire will ask his partner for help. If the call is "No, he didn't go" then the original call of ball four prevails. However, if the call is "Yes, he went," the base umpire will *emphatically* call the appeal ("Yes, he went") and then the umpire at second will turn and *very emphatically* call the runner out or safe at second base, depending on what he observed when the play occurred at second.

1.13 BASE COACHES

Do not begin an inning unless both base coaches of the offensive team have taken their positions on the field.

1.14 COACH POSITIONED OUT OF COACHING BOX

It has been common practice for many years for some coaches to put one foot outside the coach's box or stand astride or otherwise be slightly outside the coaching box lines. The coach shall not be considered out of the box unless the opposing manager complains, and then the umpire shall strictly enforce the rule and require all coaches (on both teams) to remain in the coach's box at all times.

It is also common practice for a coach who has a play at his base to leave the coach's box to signal the player to slide, advance, or return to a base. This may be allowed if the coach does not interfere with the play in any manner.

1.15 FIRST BASEMAN PLAYING IN FOUL TERRITORY

Do not insist on the first baseman playing with both feet in fair territory unless the offensive team protests. If they do, you must enforce the rule as written, but make sure it is enforced for both teams.

1.16 GOLF GLOVES

No pitcher shall be allowed to wear a golf glove while pitching. Other defensive players may wear a golf glove on their glove hand, but they shall not rub the ball with the golf glove on their hand.

1.17 WRIST BANDS; JEWELRY

Players should not wear white wrist bands while at bat or in the field.

Players, especially pitchers, will not be allowed to wear distracting jewelry of any kind.

1.18 SHOES

Players shall not wear shoes with pointed spikes similar to golf or track shoes. Excessive or distracting flaps on shoes, particularly those on pitchers, will not be allowed. Players may not call time to change shoes upon becoming a base runner.

1.19 BATS

As of 1997, the Official Playing Rules Committee has approved a total of fourteen (14) bats for use in all professional leagues. The bats which are on the approved list include: *Adirondack, Barnstable Bats, Cooperstown, Glomar, Hoosier* (one-piece ash bats only), *KC Slammer, Kissimmee Sticks, Louisville, Mizuno, Nike* (formerly Cooper), *Sticks by Stan, Worth, Young Bat Co.* (Carolina Clubs), and *Zett.* The *Baum* bat has been approved for use in *Short A and Rookie Leagues only.* Note that the *Hoosier* three-piece bat has **not** been approved for use during a game; only the *Hoosier* one-piece ash bat has been approved.

Should a player use or attempt to use a bat which is not on the above approved list of bats, the umpire is to handle the matter as described in Section 1.8 of this manual (i.e., in the same manner as a "pine-tar bat").

Colored bats have not been approved by the Official Playing Rules Committee, and therefore, the only approved colors for bats are natural grain, black, and dark wood-stained color. Other bats that have not been approved for use in professional leagues include: laminated, impregnated, or lacquered bats.

Should a player use or attempt to use a bat which does not conform to the specifications found in Official Playing Rules 1.10(a), (b), (c), or (d), such infraction shall cause the bat to be removed from the game. The player would not normally be declared out or ejected for using such a bat *unless*, in the umpire's judgment, such bat has been *altered* or *tampered with* as described in Official Playing Rule 6.06(d) (i.e., if the distance or reaction factor has been affected). (See Sections 1.8 and 1.20 in this manual.)

1.20 ALTERED OR TAMPERED BATS

Official Rule 6.06(d) provides that the batter be declared out and ejected from the game if he **uses or attempts to use** a bat that has been altered or tampered with in such a way as to improve the distance factor or cause an unusual reaction to the ball. This rule applies to bats that have been corked, filled, flat-surfaced, nailed, hollowed, grooved, or covered with a substance such as paraffin or wax. This rule does not apply to bats which have pine tar extending beyond the 18-inch limit. (See Section 1.8, "Pine Tar on Bat.")

The phrase, "**uses or attempts to use**" shall be interpreted as one pitch being delivered to the batter.

The umpire should stop a batter from using an **obviously** illegal bat if he notices it before the batter uses the bat. This would include bats which violate Official Rule 6.06(d) as well as bats that do not conform to Official Rule 1.10.

In cases of actual violation of Official Rule 6.06(d), the batter shall be declared out and ejected from the game. Umpires are to remove the illegal bat from the game and place it in a secure area for the duration of the game. The bat is then to be forwarded to the league president within twenty-four hours. The offending player shall be subject to additional penalties as determined by the league president.

In cases where a questionable bat is brought to the attention of the umpires and the umpires are not able to determine if in fact the bat is illegal, the following procedure is to be observed: The umpires shall remove the bat under question from the game and place it in a secure area for the duration of the game. The bat shall then be forwarded to the league president within twenty-four hours for further investigation by the league president. Upon further investigation, the league president has the power to impose such penalties as he deems justified. Note in this situation that although the bat is removed from the game, this shall **NOT** cause the batter to be declared out or ejected from the game.

1.21 CATCHER'S MITT

The catcher may use a mitt with a vinyl fluorescent piece attached.

1.22 FOUL TIPS

Regarding the definition of a foul tip, the interpretation to be made is that a foul tip must be caught by the catcher.

1.23 DRAGGING INFIELD

In ball parks that drag the infield during the course of the game, clubs should be instructed that the infield should not be dragged until the completion of the fifth inning. The umpire-in-chief has the authority to forbid the dragging of the infield if, in his judgment, the completion of the game may be in jeopardy by the action.

1.24 ORGANISTS; SCOREBOARDS

Clubs should instruct their organists not to play when the ball is about to be put in play. The organ should stop playing as soon as the hitter is in the batter's box and the pitcher is on the rubber. Organists are not to play in a manner that will incite spectators to react in a negative fashion to umpires' decisions.

For the purpose of this rule, the word "organist" shall include coverage of other music in the park, the public address announcer, and the scoreboard operator.

If violation of this rule occurs during the game, the umpire may have a **warning** issued to the violator. Following the first warning from the umpire, the second violation can result in the umpire dismissing the violator from his or her duties for the remainder of the game. League presidents, upon receiving an umpire's report of said situation, would then have authority to fine the club that employs the violator. Any appeal on such a situation would follow normal league procedures.

Umpires are advised not to be overly technical in the enforcement of this regulation. Good common sense should be used by all parties concerned.

1.25 TEAM MASCOTS

Team mascots are not to interfere in any manner with the duties of the umpires during the progress of the game. This would include—but is not limited to—approaching the umpires during or between innings while making motions intended to reflect upon the integrity of the umpires. This would also include approaching the umpires and inciting, or trying to incite, by word or sign a demonstration by spectators.

If a team mascot intends to involve an umpire into his "act" in any manner, this should be cleared with the umpiring crew before the start of the game.

1.26 ROVING COACHES AND INSTRUCTORS

So-called "roving" or traveling coaches and instructors are allowed on the team's bench or bullpen during the game provided that they are in full uniform (uniform of the parent Major League club is permissible).

Only if league regulations permit may such traveling personnel be allowed to take an active part in the game and/or enter the playing surface during a game. In such cases he *must* be in the uniform of the Minor League team.

Traveling coaches and instructors should not address or complain to the umpires during the game, as their purpose at the game is that of player development, and their presence on the team bench is that of a courtesy.

Should the coach/instructor violate any of these provisions, he may, **after being warned**, be removed from the game by the umpire.

SECTION 2

LINEUPS AND SUBSTITUTIONS

2.1 BATTING ORDER CARDS

The home club manager, coach, or representative must first deliver his batting order, in duplicate form as furnished by the league (some leagues are in triplicate), to the umpire-in-chief. As soon as this batting order is delivered, the umpires are in charge of the playing field, and from that moment they shall have sole authority to determine when a game shall be called, suspended, or resumed on account of weather or the condition of the playing field.

Next, the visiting club manager, coach, or representative shall deliver his batting order, in duplicate (or triplicate) form as furnished by the league, to the umpire-in-chief. The visiting club manager or representative does not have the right to examine the home club's batting order until he has given the plate umpire his batting order.

The umpire-in-chief shall then make certain that the original and copies of the respective batting orders are identical and that there are no obvious errors in either batting order. After he has determined that the copies are identical and that there are no obvious errors, he shall hand each manager copies of the batting orders. The umpire shall retain the original of each team's batting order, and these shall be considered official.

If either manager takes out a player after receiving his copy of the batting order, the player so removed cannot thereafter appear in that game.

2.2 ERRORS IN BATTING ORDER

Obvious errors in the batting order which are noticed by the umpire-in-chief before he calls "Play" for the start of the game should be called to the attention of the manager of the team in error so the correction can be made before the game starts. For example, if a manager has inadvertently listed only eight men in the batting order or has listed two players with the same last name but without an identifying initial and the errors are noticed by the umpire before he calls "Play," he shall cause such error or errors to be corrected before he calls "Play" to start the game. Teams should not be "trapped" later by some mistake that obviously was inadvertent and which can be corrected before the game starts.

2.3 BATTING OUT OF TURN

In batting out of order situations, there are two fundamentals to keep in mind:

1. When a player bats out of turn, the **proper** batter is the player called out.

2. When an improper batter becomes a runner or is put out and a pitch is made to the next batter of either team (or a play or attempted play is made) before an appeal is made, the improper batter is thereby **legalized**, and the results of his time at bat become legal. The batting order then picks up with the name following the legalized improper batter.

Any advance or outs made because of an improper batter becoming a runner would be nullified if the defensive team appeals at the proper time. (Outs made because of a pick off or out attempting to steal while the improper batter is at bat are legal.) Play is to revert back to the position of the runners at the time the improper batter took his position in the batter's box (with the exception of advances covered in the Note of Official Rule 6.07(b) or outs made on a pick off or steal play while the improper batter is at bat).

EXAMPLES:

1. Runners on first and third. Charles bats in place of Baker. Charles grounds to short; runner forced at second; Charles beats relay to first; runner on third scores. An appeal is made.

   Ruling: Baker is declared out. Runners return to first and third. Charles is next batter.

2. Runners on first and third. Charles bats in place of Baker. Charles grounds to short; runner forced at second; Charles is out at first for double play; runner on third scores. An appeal is made.

   Ruling: Baker is declared out. Runners return to first and third. Charles is next batter.

Umpires are reminded that the *only* way the defense may gain an **out** in a batting out of order situation is for the defense to appeal **immediately after** an improper batter has completed his turn at bat and **before** a pitch is made to the next batter. The reason for this is because any time a pitch is made to the next batter after an improper batter has batted, the improper batter that has just batted immediately becomes legal at that moment, and the batting order then picks up with the name following that improper batter (who has just batted and who has now become legal).

11

Consider the following example where the correct batting order is A-B-C-D-E-F-G-H-I, and, for some reason, a team is batting in the order A-B-D-C-E-F-G-H-I. That is, C and D are batting in reversed order throughout the game:

> If the batting-out-of-order error is not brought to the umpire's attention, play will proceed throughout the game without reference to the batting out of order. However, suppose one inning that B is the correct lead-off batter and gets a base hit. D then comes to bat. D is an improper batter, and if this error is brought to the attention of the umpire while D is at bat, C will replace D with the count then on D (no penalty).

> However, suppose that the defense does not appeal during D's at-bat and D gets a base hit, which puts B on second and D on first. If the defense now appeals before the next pitch (or play or attempted play), C—who was the **proper** batter—is declared out, B returns to first base, and D is now the next batter.

> However, if nothing is said after D's base hit and one pitch is thrown to C, this immediately legalizes D's actions (the batter who just batted), and now the proper batter is E. If the defense appeals while C is batting (i.e., after one or more pitches have been thrown to C), E shall then come to bat with the count then on C.

> However, suppose that no appeal is made while C is at bat and C gets on base to load the bases (B is now on third, D on second, and C on first). If the defense now appeals, note that the first pitch to the last batter (C) legalized the man who appeared at bat just before him (D). That made E (the name following D in the lineup) the proper batter. Since C has just completed an at-bat (instead of E), and since the defense is appealing before the next pitch, E is then declared out, B returns to second, D returns to first, and F is the next batter.

> Suppose, however, that no appeal is made after C's at-bat, and the next batter to appear at bat is E. If one pitch is thrown to E, this immediately legalizes the actions of the batter who just appeared at bat (C). So now if the defense appeals (after one or more pitches to E), the proper batter would be D. However, since D is already on base, the rules provide that we skip over his name and go on to E, who is already currently at bat anyway. In that situation, E has now become the proper batter, and the original batting order would continue on from that point.

The preceding example may seem somewhat complicated, but the key to unraveling all batting out of order situations is again to remember the following three points:

1. In order to gain an out in a batting out of order, the defense must appeal *immediately* after an improper batter has completed his turn at bat and before the next pitch (or play or attempted play).

2. If the defense does appeal at the correct moment, the **proper** batter is always the player called out.

3. Any time an improper batter completes a time at bat and a pitch is then made to the next batter, the improper batter (who has just batted) immediately becomes legal at that moment, and the batting order then picks up with the name following that *improper* batter (who has now become the proper batter).

Another way of looking at this last point is to remember the following statements: As soon as a pitch is made to a batter, the man who batted just before him always becomes legal, even if he was an improper batter to begin with. The correct next batter will then be the name which follows the man who has just finished his at-bat.

There is one final and very important point for umpires to remember concerning batting out of order: *If the defense appeals that there has been a batting out of order, the umpire need only concern himself with the __last two batters__.* The reason for this is that we know that no matter who just batted, the man who batted immediately before him was **legal** (proper). Therefore, the correct last batter will always be the name which follows the man who batted immediately before this last batter.

2.4   DESIGNATED HITTER

The designated hitter listed in the starting lineup must complete at least one time at bat (is put out or becomes a base runner) unless the opposing club changes pitchers.

Once the game pitcher bats for the designated hitter, this move shall terminate the designated hitter's role for the remainder of the game. (The only person the game pitcher may pinch hit for is the designated hitter.)

If a **designated hitter** assumes a defensive position, this move shall terminate the designated hitter's role for the remainder of the game. Since the DH is "locked" in the batting order, the designated hitter must continue to bat in that slot. The pitcher must then bat in place of the substituted defensive player (unless more than one defensive substitution is made, and then the manager must designate their spots in the batting order to the umpire).

If a **game pitcher** is switched from the mound to a defensive position, this move shall terminate the designated hitter's role for the remainder of the game. The pitcher just removed from the mound may bat in the DH spot in the batting order; or, if more than one defensive change is made, the pitcher may bat in place of any one of the substituted players (manager shall designate to the umpire).

It is permissible for both the **designated hitter and the game pitcher** to go into the field at the same time (i.e., the game pitcher switches from the mound to a defensive position **and** the DH goes into the field). Such a move will terminate the designated hitter role for the remainder of that game. Since the DH is "locked" in the batting order, the designated hitter must continue to bat in that slot. The pitcher then bats in place of any one of the substituted defensive players (manager shall designate to the umpire).

If a defensive player goes to the mound (i.e., replaces the game pitcher), this move shall terminate the designated hitter's role for the remainder of the game.

The designated hitter may not serve as a pinch runner.

A substitute for the designated hitter need not be announced until it is the designated hitter's turn to bat.

The designated hitter may not sit in the bullpen unless he is serving as a catcher in the bullpen.

2.5 MAKING SUBSTITUTIONS

A player or players may be substituted during a game at any time the ball is dead.

The manager shall immediately notify the umpire-in-chief of any substitution and shall state to the umpire-in-chief the substitute's place in his batting order.

A substitution is completed and the player considered as having entered the game when the manager notifies the umpire-in-chief of such substitution. If no such notification is given or if after notification no announcement is made, the player shall be considered as having entered the game when:

1. If a pitcher, he takes his place on the pitcher's plate prior to delivering a pitch (preparatory or otherwise);

2. If a batter, he takes his place in the batter's box;

3. If a fielder, he reaches the position usually occupied by the fielder he has replaced, **and play commences**;

4. If a runner, he takes the place of the runner he has replaced.

Umpires are instructed to confirm **all** substitutes from the manager and to inform the opposing manager of same.

When the umpire-in-chief is informed by the manager of a substitution, he is to make the change on his lineup card. Then he is to point out the substitution to the press box by first holding his hand up to the press box and then pointing to the substitute player's position on the field. The opposing manager should also be informed of the substitution. The substitution should not be pointed out until *after* the umpire has made the change on his lineup card.

2.6   MULTIPLE SUBSTITUTIONS

When two or more substitute players of the defensive team enter the game at the same time, the manager shall, immediately **before** they take their positions as fielders, designate to the umpire-in-chief such players' positions in the team's batting order and the umpire-in-chief shall so notify the official scorer. If this information is not **immediately** given to the umpire-in-chief, he shall have authority to designate the substitutes' places in the batting order.

In making two or more defensive substitutions at the same time, the manager must advise, **at the same moment**, the umpire-in-chief the names of the substitutes, their defensive positions, and in what place each will hit in the batting order. The manager cannot give notice of one of the substitutions, leave the umpire, come back to the umpire-in-chief, and locate the other player in the lineup. In case the manager fails or refuses to make a decision, the umpire-in-chief is authorized to decide the necessary batting order changes, and his decision is final. Just as soon as the substitutes are legal, this information must be announced to the press box, announcements should be made over the P.A. system, and the opposing manager should be informed.

If a manager wishes to change pitchers along with one or more other defensive players (intending to interchange the batting order), he must inform the umpire **before** calling for the new pitcher. Motioning to the bullpen is to be considered an official substitution for the new pitcher.

It is **not** permissible for the manager to go to the mound, call for a new pitcher, and **then** inform the umpire of multiple substitutions with the intention of interchanging the batting order. The umpire-in-chief **must** be informed of the multiple substitutions **before** the manager calls for a new pitcher (if the manager wishes to interchange the batting order).

If two or more defensive substitutions are made at the same time, make certain that the press box is clearly informed as to the substitutes' positions in the batting order. This should be done using the "flip-flop" signal or the "straight up" signal to the press box after pointing out the substitutions. Sometimes the umpire may have to verbally and visually announce to the press box what position a particular substitute is batting in. For example, if several substitutions have been made, the umpire may have to announce to the press box, "New pitcher is batting fifth," while holding up five fingers to the press box after pointing to the pitcher.

Once again, also make certain that the opposing manager is always informed of multiple substitutions and is given the proper batting position of each substitution.

2.7   UNANNOUNCED SUBSTITUTES

If a player's name appears in the original batting order and before he appears at bat, another player takes this player's position on the field or at bat and no notification is made to the umpire, the player shall be considered as entering the game only as a substitute player. This is not a batting out of order situation where the opposing manager could protest later in the game. As provided in Official Rule 3.08(b), any play or any hit made by such unannounced substitute would be legal.

2.8   SUBSTITUTE FOR INJURED OR DISABLED PLAYER

Any player (other than a pitcher) who is substituted for an injured or disabled player shall be allowed five warm-up throws. (See Official Rule 8.03 for pitchers.)

SECTION 3

APPEALS AND AWARDS

3.1 PLAY OR ATTEMPTED PLAY

A key phrase in both the awarding of bases (Official Rule 7.05(g)) and in appeal plays (Official Rule 7.10) is "play or attempted play." Note the following official interpretation:

A **play or attempted play** (Official Rules 7.05(g) and 7.10) shall be interpreted as a legitimate effort by a defensive player who has possession of the ball to actually retire a runner. This may include an actual attempt to tag a runner, a fielder running toward a base with the ball in an attempt to force or tag a runner, or actually throwing to another defensive player in an attempt to retire a runner. A fake or a feint to throw shall not be deemed a play or an attempted play. (The fact that the runner is not out is not relevant.)

EXAMPLES:

A play or attempted play:

1. Runners on first and second, ground ball to the shortstop who makes a swipe at the runner from second but misses and then throws beyond first base into the stands. The swipe by the shortstop is an attempted play; thus the throw to first is not the first play by an infielder (even though it is the first throw), and the proper award of bases would be from the time of the throw.

2. Runner on first and ground ball to second baseman who flips ball to short to get runner from first but who is **safe**. Shortstop throws beyond first into the stands. The flip by the second baseman to the shortstop is an attempted play, even though unsuccessful. The throw to first is not the first play by an infielder and thus runner should be placed from the time of the throw. Runner who was on first would score and batter-runner would be placed at second.

Not a play or attempted play:

1. A fake or a feint to a base but not actually throwing, even though the fielder draws his arm back to feint a throw.

2. A pitcher feinting a throw toward a base to hold or check a runner's progress in order to complete an appeal play at another base.

17

3. Runner on first, ground ball to the shortstop, who starts to flip the ball to the second baseman but doesn't and throws the ball beyond first and out of play. The feint to the second baseman is not considered a play or attempted play and award of bases is from the time of the pitch.

4. Runners on first and third, runner on first stealing as ground ball is hit to shortstop. The shortstop feints a throw home but does not throw—instead throws to first and into the stands; during this the runner from first has rounded second base.

The feint by the shortstop toward home is not considered a play or attempted play; thus his throw beyond first is the first play by an infielder and awards should be made from the time of the pitch.

3.2 APPEAL PLAYS

Keep the following points in mind regarding appeal plays:

1. Any appeal under Official Rule 7.10 must be made before the next pitch or any play or attempted play. (See Section 3.1, "Play or Attempted Play.")

2. If a pitcher balks when making an appeal, such act shall be considered a play. No further appeal will be allowed.

3. If the pitcher or any member of the defensive team throws the ball out of play when making an appeal, such act shall be considered an attempted play. No further appeal will be allowed. (This refers to when an appeal is being made after a definite break in action.)

4. If the violation occurs during a play which ends a half-inning, the appeal must be made before the defensive team leaves the field (pitcher and all infielders have crossed the foul lines).

5. An appeal is not to be interpreted as a play or an attempted play.

6. An appeal should be clearly intended as an appeal, either by a verbal request by the player or an act that unmistakably indicates an appeal to the umpire.

3.3 RUNNER MISSES HOME PLATE

Should a runner in scoring fail to touch home plate and continue on his way to the bench, he may be put out by the fielder touching home plate and appealing to the umpire for a decision. However, this rule applies only where a runner is on his way to the bench and the catcher would be required to chase him. It does not apply to the ordinary play where the runner misses the plate and then immediately makes an effort to touch the plate before being tagged. In that case, the runner must be tagged.

On a play at the plate, should the runner miss home plate and the fielder miss the tag on the runner, the umpire shall make **no signal** on the play. As outlined in the previous paragraph, the runner must then be tagged if he attempts to return to the plate; if he continues on his way to the bench, the defense may make an appeal.

3.4 APPEAL PLAYS—APPROVED RULINGS

The following are approved rulings concerning appeal plays:

1. Runner on first, one out. The batter doubles. Runner on first rounds the bases and tries for home. On the play at the plate, the catcher misses the tag and runner misses the plate as he slides by. As the catcher begins to chase the runner to apply a tag, the batter-runner tries for third base. Seeing this, the catcher throws to the third baseman, who retires the batter-runner. Can the defensive team still appeal at home on the runner originally on first?

   Ruling: Yes. The catcher's play on the batter-runner at third base was still part of the continuous action created by and following the batted ball. Therefore, the defensive team would not lose its rights to make an appeal by playing on the runner at home or the batter-runner at third and may still appeal at home.

2. Runner on first base, one out. The pitcher attempts a pick off but throws the ball past the first baseman down the right field line. Runner misses second base but tries for third. The right fielder's throw to get the runner at third base is too late, although he is tagged by the third baseman. Can the defense appeal at second base that the runner missed it?

   Ruling: Yes. The third baseman's attempted play on the runner at third base was still part of the continuous action created by and following the aborted pick off throw. Therefore, the defensive team does not lose its right to make its appeal by playing on the runner at third base and may still appeal.

3. Runners on first and third, two out. The pitcher's next pitch is a wild pitch back to the screen. While the ball is being chased down, the runner on third crosses the plate. Runner from first misses second base but tries for third. The catcher's throw to third base gets past the third baseman, and runner tries to score. The shortstop, backing up third, attempts to throw the runner out at the plate, but the catcher's tag is too late, and the runner is ruled safe. Can

the defensive team still appeal at second base on the runner originally on first?

Ruling: Yes. The defensive team's attempted plays on the runner originally on first at third and home were still part of the continuous action created by and following the wild pitched ball. Therefore, the defensive team does not lose its right to make its appeal by attempting these plays and may still appeal on the runner originally on first at second base.

4. Runner on first, one out. The batter singles. Runner from first misses second base and advances to third without a play. The ball comes into the infield and is returned to the pitcher. The pitcher stretches, comes to a set position, and then legally steps off the rubber to start an appeal at second base. The original runner from first (now on third) breaks for home as the defense starts its appeal. The pitcher, instead of completing his appeal play, throws home to get the runner, but the tag is too late, and he is ruled safe. Can the defensive team still appeal at second base?

Ruling: No. The defensive team's attempt to retire the original runner at home occurred after a definite break in the original continuous action that was created by and followed the batted ball. Therefore, the defensive team lost its right to make any appeals once it made the play at home and may not appeal.

5. Runner on first, one out. Runner from first goes to third on a single but misses second base. Runner is safe at third on a sliding tag play. The ball is returned to the pitcher, who steps on the rubber, stretches, and comes to a set position. The defense intends to appeal, but the pitcher balks as he steps off the rubber. After the penalty is enforced, can the defense still appeal at second base on the original runner from first?

Ruling: No. The defense did not lose its right to appeal by playing on the runner originally on first at third base; that play was still part of the continuous action created by and following the batted ball. However, a balk is considered a play for the purpose of this section of the appeal rule. Since the defensive team cannot appeal following a play or attempted play, the pitcher's balk cost the defensive team its right to make an appeal.

6. Runner on second, one out. Runner from second attempts to score on a single but misses third base. Runner is safe at home on a sliding tag play. On the throw home, the batter-runner tries to take

second and is safe there on a sliding tag play, as the catcher's throw is too late to retire him. Time is called. The pitcher steps on the rubber, stretches, and comes to a set position. The defense intends to appeal at third on the runner originally on second. The pitcher legally steps back off the rubber, checks the runner at second base, and steps to throw to third for the appeal. The pitcher's throw, however, is wild and goes into dead territory beyond the third baseman. The runner on second is properly awarded home. Can the defense still make its intended appeal at third on the runner originally on second when a new ball is put into play?

Ruling: No. The attempted plays to retire the runner originally on second at home and the batter-runner at second occurred during the continuous action which was created by and followed the batted ball and do not nullify the defensive team's right to make an appeal. However, once the defensive team "errs" (i.e., throws the ball out of play) in its attempt to appeal at third on the runner originally on second, it loses its right to make an appeal. Throwing the ball out of play in this situation is considered an attempted play which occurred after a definite break in the continuous action play.

7. No runners. The batter doubles but misses first base. Time is called. The pitcher steps on the rubber, stretches, and comes to a set position. The defense intends to appeal at first base. The pitcher legally steps off the rubber and checks the runner at second base. The pitcher's throw for the appeal gets past the first baseman but remains in play. The runner advances to third as the ball is being retrieved. Can the defensive team still make its intended appeal at first base?

Ruling: Yes. Since the ball is live and in play, if the ball is retrieved and thrown back to first base immediately, the appeal is allowed.

8. Runner on first, one out. The batter singles. Runner on first misses second base but is safe at third on sliding tag play. Time is called. The pitcher steps on the rubber, stretches, and comes to a set position. The defense intends to appeal at second base. The pitcher legally steps off the rubber. Seeing this, the runner originally on first (now on third) bluffs as if to go home. The pitcher, now off the rubber, steps toward third and cocks his arm as if to throw but does not throw. Can the defensive team still make its intended appeal at second base on the runner originally on first?

Ruling: Yes. The attempted play at third on the runner originally on first was still part of the continuous action created by and fol-

21

lowing the batted ball and therefore did not nullify the defensive team's right to make an appeal. The bluff by the pitcher (step and cocked arm) to check the runner at third is **not** considered a play or attempted play. Therefore, the defensive team may still attempt its intended appeal at second base.

9. Runner on first, one out. Batter hits home run out of ball park. Runner from first misses second and batter-runner misses first. After both runners cross the plate, the umpire puts new ball in play. Pitcher takes his position on the rubber, steps off, and intends to make an appeal at first base on the batter-runner. However, his throw is wild and goes into the stands. The umpire then puts another ball into play, and the pitcher again takes his position on the rubber and steps off. This time he intends to make an appeal at second base on the runner originally on first. Should the umpire allow the appeal?

Ruling: No. If the pitcher throws the ball out of play when making an appeal, such act shall be considered an attempted play. No further appeal will be allowed.

10. Runners on first and third, one out. Runner from first is stealing on the pitch. Batter hits a fly ball to right field which is caught for the second out. Runner on third tags and scores after the catch. Runner from first tries to return to first base after the catch, but the right fielder's throw beats him to the bag and he is declared out for the third out of the inning. Runner from third base touched home plate before the third out was made at first base.

Ruling: Run counts. **This is a time play, NOT a force play**.

3.5   FIELDER FALLING INTO DUGOUT OR STANDS

If a fielder after catching a fly ball falls down in the dugout, or falls into a dugout, bench, or stand at any point while in possession of the ball, the base runner(s) shall be entitled to advance one base and the ball shall be dead.

3.6   "TIME OF PITCH"

The **time of pitch** is defined as the moment the pitcher's movements commit him to deliver the ball to the batter.

- In a windup position, this is defined as the moment the pitcher begins the natural movement associated with his delivery of the ball to the batter (i.e., the start of his windup or delivery).

- From a set position, this is defined as the moment the pitcher begins the natural movement associated with his delivery of the ball to the batter *after* the pitcher has come set with both hands together in front of his body.

A runner who advances while the pitcher is in contact with the rubber is considered to occupy the base last touched at the time the pitcher initiates his actual pitching motion to the batter. The pitching motion is defined as any movement which commits the pitcher to deliver the ball to the batter.

As long as the pitcher is not committed to pitch, a runner may advance and is considered to occupy the last base touched at the time the pitcher initiates his actual delivery to the batter.

The preliminary motion known as the "stretch" is **not** considered the start of the pitching motion.

3.7   AWARDING BASES ON WILD THROWS

See Official Rule 7.05(g) regarding awarding of bases on balls that are thrown out of play. In making such awards, keep the following points in mind:

1. If throw is first play by infielder and batter-runner has **not** reached first base when throw was made, award all runners from **time of pitch**.

2. If throw is first play by infielder **and** all runners including the batter-runner **have** advanced a base when throw was made, award all runners from **time of throw**.

3. If throw is **not** first play by infielder or the throw is made by outfielder, award all runners from **time of throw**.

The Approved Ruling of Official Rule 7.05(g) provides that when the first throw is by an infielder **after** runners and batter have advanced one base, then runners are awarded two bases from their position when the throw was made. (See Item 2 above.) This can happen on a high fly that an infielder goes back to catch but drops the ball during which time the batter and runners have clearly advanced one base; then in an attempt to put out the batter-runner after he has passed first base, he throws the ball into the stands. While it is the first throw by an infielder, the runners, including the batter-runner, had advanced one base before the throw and accordingly are awarded two bases from the base they last touched when the throw was made. Before awarding two bases from the base last touched by the runners, the umpire must judge that all the runners have definitely advanced to the next base before the throw was made.

The term "when the wild throw was made" means when the throw actually left the player's hand and not when the thrown ball hit the ground, passes a receiving fielder, or goes out of play into the stands.

When a runner is awarded bases without liability to be put out because the ball has gone out of play, he is not relieved of his responsibility to touch the base he is awarded and all intervening bases. (See Section 3.10 regarding returning to missed bases when the ball is dead.)

3.8 BALLS DEFLECTED OUT OF PLAY

If a pitched ball deflects off the catcher and goes **directly** out of play, the award is **one base from the time of the pitch**.

If a ball thrown by the pitcher while in contact with the rubber deflects off a fielder and goes **directly** out of play, the award is **one base** from the time of the **throw**.

If a pitched ball goes through or by the catcher and remains on the playing field and is **subsequently kicked or deflected** out of play (unintentionally in either case), the award is **two bases** from the time of the **pitch**. If a ball thrown by the pitcher while in contact with the rubber goes through or by a fielder and remains on the playing field and is **subsequently kicked or deflected** out of play, the award is **two bases** from the time of the throw. The phrase, *"remains on the playing field and is subsequently kicked or deflected out of play"* is interpreted to mean that the **impetus of the fielder caused the ball to go out of play** (for example, the ball has come to rest and is then deflected out of play; or the ball is not rolling towards an out-of-play area but the deflection causes it to go out of play). If the umpire judges that the deflected ball would have gone out of play on its own, the award in such situations is **one base**. On the other hand, if the umpire judges that the deflection in fact caused the ball to go out of play (and it would not have gone out of play had the fielder not touched it), then the award is **two bases**.

EXAMPLES:

1. With runners on base, a pitched ball deflects off the catcher and rolls towards the dugout. It is obvious that the ball *will* roll into the dugout on its own. The catcher, chasing after the ball, dives and tries to stop the ball from entering the dugout. The ball deflects off the catcher's outstretched gloved hand and rolls into the dugout anyway.

   Ruling: One base from the time of the pitch.

2. With runners on base, a wild pitch goes past the catcher and strikes the backstop. The ball rebounds and rolls towards an out-of-play line. It is obvious that the ball *will* roll out of play on its own. The catcher, chasing after the ball, dives and tries to stop the ball from going out of play. The ball deflects off the catcher's outstretched gloved hand and rolls out of play anyway.

   Ruling: One base from the time of the pitch.

3. With runners on base, a wild pitch goes past the catcher and strikes the backstop. The ball rebounds and rolls back towards home plate. The catcher, chasing after the ball, tries to field the ball but inadvertently kicks (or deflects) the ball into the dugout.

Ruling: Two bases from the time of the pitch.

If a thrown ball deflects off a fielder and goes **directly** out of play, the award is two bases from the time of the pitch if it is the first play by an infielder; otherwise the award is two bases from the time of the throw. (See Section 3.7, "Awarding Bases on Wild Throws.")

If a thrown ball goes through or by a fielder and remains on the playing field and is **subsequently kicked or deflected out of play**, the award is two bases from the time of the throw.

If a fair fly ball is deflected in flight by a fielder and then goes out of the playing field in flight over fair territory, it is a home run.

If a fair fly ball is deflected in flight by a fielder and then goes out of play outside the foul lines, the award is two bases from the time of the pitch.

If a fair ball not in flight is deflected by a fielder and then goes out of play, the award is two bases from the time of the pitch.

If a fielder has **complete possession** of a batted or thrown ball and subsequently deflects or kicks the ball out of play, the award is two bases from the position of the runners at the time the ball was kicked or deflected.

If a fielder has **complete possession** of a batted or thrown ball and drops the ball while he is out of play, or if he drops such a ball and it then goes out of play, the award is two bases from the position of the runners at the time the ball was dropped.

If, in the judgment of the umpires, a fielder **intentionally kicks or deflects** a batted or thrown ball out of play, the award is **two bases** from the **time the ball was kicked or deflected**.

3.9 DETACHED EQUIPMENT TOUCHING PITCHED OR BATTED BALL

Any defensive player deliberately touching a **pitched ball** with detached equipment (such as a catcher's mask, cap, etc.) will entitle all runners to advance **one base** from the time the ball was touched without liability to be put out. The ball is in play, and runners may advance beyond the awarded base at their own risk.

Any defensive player deliberately touching a **batted ball over fair territory** (or a batted ball over **foul** territory which, in the umpire's judgment has an opportunity to become a fair ball) with detached equipment will entitle all runners—including the batter-runner—to advance **three bases** from the time the ball was touched without liability to be put out. The ball is in play, and runners may advance beyond the awarded base at their own risk.

3.10 RETOUCHING BASES WHEN BALL IS DEAD

When the ball is dead, no runner may return to touch a missed base or one he has left too soon after he has advanced to and touched a base beyond the missed base. A runner may return to a missed base (or one he has left too soon) when the ball is dead if he has not touched the next base. A runner may, of course, return to any missed base (or one he has left too soon) while the ball is in play unless a following runner has scored.

EXAMPLES:

1. Batter hits ball out of park or ground rule double and misses first base (ball is dead). He may return to first base to correct his mistake before he touches second; but if he touches second, he may not return to first; and if defensive team appeals, he is declared out at first.

2. Batter hits ball to shortstop who throws wild into stands (ball is dead). Batter-runner misses first base but is awarded second base on the overthrow. Even though the umpire has awarded the runner second base on the overthrow, the runner must return to touch first base before he touches second base.

3. Batter hits single to right field and misses first base in rounding it. Right fielder makes quick throw to first baseman in an attempt to pick off batter-runner before he can return to first base. However, his throw is wild and goes into dugout.

   Ruling: Batter-runner is awarded third base. However, he must return to and touch first base before he touches second. While the ball is dead, he may return to first base to correct his mistake before he touches second; but if he touches second he may not return to first, and if the defensive team appeals, he is declared out at first.

3.11 AWARD MADE FROM ORIGINAL BASE AFTER CATCH

If a runner is forced to return to a base after a catch, he must retouch his original base even though, because of some ground rule or other rule, he is awarded additional bases. He may retouch while the ball is dead, and the award is made from his original base.

EXAMPLES:

1. Runner on first, one out. Hit and run. Batter hits a line drive to the shortstop, who catches the ball for the second out. Shortstop's throw to first is wild and goes into the stands. Runner originally on first is between first and second when wild throw is made.

Ruling: Runner originally on first is awarded third. However, while the ball is dead, he must return to and retouch first base before he touches second on his way to third. If he touches second he may not return to first, and if the defensive team appeals he is declared out at first.

2. Runner on first, one out. Batter flies out to right field for second out. However, runner on first thought there were two out and is between second and third when the ball is caught. Right fielder's throw to first is wild and goes into dugout. Runner is between second and third when ball goes out of play.

Ruling: Runner is awarded third (two bases from his original base). However, while the ball is dead, he must return to and retouch first base. Furthermore, since he was between second and third when the ball went out of play, he must return to first before he reaches and touches third (the next base). If he touches third, he may not return to first; and if the defensive team appeals, he is out at first.

3.12 DEFENSE MUST APPEAL ORIGINAL BASE AFTER CATCH

When a runner misses a base and a fielder holds the ball on the missed base, or on the base **originally occupied** by the runner if a fly ball is caught, and appeals for the umpire's decision, the runner is out when the umpire sustains the appeal.

Play: Runner on first, batter hits the ball far into the outfield and runner races for third. Catch is made, and outfielder throws ball to shortstop who steps on second base asking umpire to rule an out. This is improper play by the shortstop, as runner may be called out only by being tagged or first base being touched before the runner reaches first base.

3.13 RUNNER FORCED HOME ALLOWED TO SCORE AFTER THIRD OUT

A runner forced to advance without liability to be put out may advance past the base to which he is entitled only at his peril. If such a runner, forced to advance, is put out for the third out before a preceding runner, also forced to advance, touches home plate, the run shall score.

Play: Two out, bases full, batter walks, but runner from second is overzealous and runs past third base toward home and is tagged out on a throw by the catcher. Even though two are out, the run would score on the theory that the run was forced home by the base on balls and that all the runners needed to do was proceed and touch the next base.

3.14 ABANDONING BASE PATHS

Any runner after reaching first base who leaves the baseline heading for his dugout or his position believing that there is no further play, may be declared out if the umpire judges the act of the runner to be considered abandoning his efforts to run the bases. Even though an out is called, the ball remains in play in regard to any other runner.

This rule also covers the following and similar plays: Less than two out; score tied last of ninth inning; runner on first; batter hits a ball out of park for winning run; runner on first passes second and, thinking the home run automatically wins the game, cuts across diamond toward his bench as batter-runner circles bases. In this case, the base runner would be called out for "abandoning his effort to touch the next base" and batter-runner permitted to continue around bases to make his home run valid. If there are two out, home run would not count. (See Official Rule 7.12.) This is not an appeal play.

Play: Bases loaded, two out, score tied in bottom of the ninth inning. Batter hits home run out of ball park. Runner on first, thinking home run automatically wins the game, leaves the baseline and heads toward dugout. He is declared out before the runner from third reaches home plate. Other runners continue around the bases and eventually touch home.

Ruling: No runs score; this is a time play. Game continues in the top of the tenth inning with the score still tied.

3.15 PASSING A PRECEDING RUNNER

Any runner is out when he passes a preceding runner before such runner is out.

Play: Bases loaded, two out. Batter hits home run out of ball park but passes runner on first **before** runner on third reaches the plate. All runners continue around the bases and touch home.

Ruling: No runs score; this is a time play. (Note clarification to Official Rule 4.11(c)—Approved Ruling.)

3.16 PUTTING NEW BALL IN PLAY AFTER HOME RUN

After a home run is hit out of the playing field, the umpire shall not deliver a new ball to the pitcher or the catcher until the batter hitting the home run has crossed the plate.

3.17 PUTTING BALL IN PLAY AFTER BALL IS DEAD

After the ball is dead, the plate umpire shall resume play by calling "Play" (pointing to the pitcher) as soon as the pitcher takes his place on the rubber with the ball in his possession and the batter has taken his position in the batter's box.

SECTION 4

INTERFERENCE AND OBSTRUCTION

4.1 OFFENSIVE INTERFERENCE

Offensive interference is an act by the team at bat which interferes with, obstructs, impedes, hinders, or confuses any fielder attempting to make a play. More specifically, if a runner fails to avoid a fielder who is attempting to field a batted ball or if a runner hinders a fielder attempting to make a play on a batted ball, the runner shall be called out for interference.

Note that under the Official Rules, a fielder is protected while he is in the act of fielding a batted ball. In addition, note that a fielder is also protected while he is in the act of making a play after he has fielded a batted ball. If a runner hinders or impedes a fielder after he has fielded a batted ball but before he is able to throw the ball, the runner shall be called out for interference. Furthermore, a runner who is adjudged to have hindered a fielder who is attempting to make a play on a batted ball is out whether it was intentional or not.

If the umpire declares the batter, batter-runner, or a runner out for interference, all other runners shall return to the last base that was, in the judgment of the umpire, legally touched at the time of the interference unless otherwise provided by the Official Rules.

Play: In a rundown between third base and home plate, the runner from second base has advanced to and is standing on third base when the runner in the rundown is called out for offensive interference.

Ruling: The umpire shall send the runner standing on third base back to second base. The reasoning is that third base legally belongs to the runner in the rundown. The following runner has not legally reached third base at the time of interference and must therefore return to second base.

Play: In a rundown between third base and home plate, the runner from first base has advanced to and is standing on second base when the runner in the rundown is called out for offensive interference.

Ruling: The umpire shall allow the runner to remain at second base. The reasoning is that on interference, all runners return to the last legally touched base at the time of interference.

4.2 INTERFERENCE WITH INTERVENING PLAY

Play: Play at the plate on runner attempting to score; runner is called safe. A following play is made on the batter-runner, and he is called out for interference outside the three-foot lane.

Ruling: With less than two out, the run scores and batter-runner is out. With two out, the run does **not** count. The reasoning is that an intervening play occurred before the interference. Runners would return to base last legally touched at time of interference. However, with two out, the runner reached home on a play in which the batter-runner was out before he reached first base. (Note this clarification to Official Rule 2.00—Interference (a) casebook comment.)

4.3 WILLFUL AND DELIBERATE INTERFERENCE

Rules 7.09(g) and 7.09(h) were inserted in the Official Baseball Rules to add an additional penalty when a base runner or a batter-runner deliberately and intentionally interferes with a batted ball or a fielder in the act of fielding a batted ball to deprive the defensive team of an opportunity to complete a possible double play. Keep in mind the rules provide that the runner or a batter-runner must interfere with the **obvious attempt to break up a double play**. A runner from third willfully running into the catcher fielding a pop fly ball, or a runner on second base deliberately running into a ground ball or allowing the ball to hit him to prevent a double play are examples that require the call of a double play under these rules.

Rule 6.05(m) was inserted in the Official Baseball Rules "to penalize the offensive team for deliberate, unwarranted, unsportsmanlike action by the runner in leaving the baseline for the obvious purpose of crashing the pivot man on a double play rather than trying to reach the base." Note the following official interpretation:

If, in the judgment of the umpire, a runner **willfully and deliberately interferes** with a fielder attempting to catch a thrown ball or attempting to throw a ball with the **obvious intent to deprive the defense of the opportunity to make a double play**, the umpire shall declare the runner out for interference and shall also declare the batter-runner out for the interference of his teammate.

In sliding to a base, the runner should be able to reach the base with his hand or foot.

EXAMPLES:

1. Bases loaded, no outs, ground ball to short stop. Anticipating a double play, runner from second intentionally crashes into short stop and grabs him just as shortstop is beginning his throw to second.

Ruling: Runner from second is guilty of willfully and deliberately interfering with a fielder with the obvious intent to deprive the defense of the opportunity to make a double play. Runner from second is declared out and so is batter-runner. Runners return to first and third.

2. Runners on first and third, no outs. Runner on first is stealing as batter hits a ground ball to shortstop. Anticipating a double play, runner from first intentionally rolls into and grabs the second baseman who is covering second and waiting for the throw from the shortstop.

   Ruling: Runner on first is guilty of willfully and deliberately interfering with a fielder with the obvious intent to deprive the defense of the opportunity to make a double play. Runner from first is declared out and so is batter-runner. Runner returns to third.

3. Bases loaded, no outs, ground ball to short stop. Shortstop's throw to second retires the runner from first. However, anticipating a double play, runner from first intentionally slides out of the base line and crashes into the second baseman just as he is beginning his throw to first base. Runner is not able to reach second base with his hand or foot.

   Ruling: Runner is guilty of willfully and deliberately interfering with a fielder with the obvious intent to deprive the defense of the opportunity to make a double play. Batter-runner is declared out for runner's interference, and runners return to second and third. Note in this example that if the runner had not been ruled out at second (i.e., if the throw pulls the fielder off the bag) and the runner had still intentionally interfered in the manner described, **both** he and the batter-runner would be declared out.

4. Runners on first and second, no outs. On hit and run play, batter hits ground ball to deep short. Runner from first makes clean slide at second and is ruled safe. However, the runner then grabs the second baseman's arm as he is throwing to first base.

   Ruling: Runner from first is out for interference. However, batter is awarded first base and runner returns to second. The runner intentionally interfered with the second baseman's throw, but he did **not** willfully and deliberately interfere with the obvious intent to deprive the defense of the opportunity to make a double play. The runner's intent in this case was to reach second safely, and subsequently he interfered with the second baseman's throw to first. Consequently, he is the only player called out on the play.

In plays of this nature, the umpire shall be governed by the **intent** of the base runner. If the umpire judges that the runner **willfully and deliberately interfered with the obvious intent to deprive the defense of the opportunity to make a double play**, he shall declare **both** the runner and batter-runner out. If this is not the case, the umpire shall declare **only** the runner out. Note, however, that if in these situations the runner has already been put out, then the runner on whom the defense was attempting a play shall be declared out. (See Section 4.4.)

4.4   INTERFERENCE BY RUNNER ALREADY PUT OUT

If any batter or runner who has just been put out hinders or impedes any following play being made on a runner, such runner shall be declared out for the interference of his teammate. The runner should be able to reach the base with his hand or foot if he is attempting to break up a double play.

4.5   BATTED BALL STRIKING THE RUNNER

The concept of the runner being in jeopardy after the ball goes past an infielder and strikes him in a situation where another infielder still has a chance to make a play on the ball applies ONLY when the ball **PASSES** the first infielder without being touched or deflected by him. This concept does **NOT APPLY** if the ball is touched or deflected by the first infielder, even though another infielder has a chance to make a play on the ball.

The reasoning for the above concept is that a runner cannot be expected to avoid a deflected ball while he is running and should not, therefore, be in jeopardy of being called out for being struck by such a deflected ball. Of course, a runner may still be guilty of intentional interference even after an infielder deflects the ball if he (the runner) deliberately deflects it or allows it to strike him when he could have reasonably avoided it. The fact that the ball has been deflected by an infielder should not be taken as a license for a runner to intentionally interfere. (See Official Rules 7.09(g) and (h).)

EXAMPLES:

1. Runner on second base, one out. The batter hits a ball on the ground toward the hole. The third baseman charges in on the grass to try to cut it off as the shortstop breaks deep toward the hole while runner is advancing. The ball gets past the third base man without being touched by him and strikes the runner in the base path. The shortstop had a play on the ball.

   Ruling: Runner from second is out and the batter-runner is awarded first base. The ball passed by but was not touched by an infielder other than the pitcher before striking the runner. However, another fielder behind the runner was deprived of an opportunity to field the ball.

2. Runner on second base, one out. The batter hits a ground ball toward the hole. The third baseman charges in on the grass to cut it off and the shortstop breaks deep toward the hole as runner advances. The ball is deflected by the third baseman in the direction of the short-stop. The shortstop would have had a play on the ball, but the ball struck the runner, resulting in no play being possible.

   Ruling: Runner from second is not out and ball is alive and in play (assuming no intentional interference by runner from second). The fact that the shortstop would have been able to have a play on the ball had it not struck the runner is disregarded because the ball was deflected by the first infielder.

3. Runner on first base, one out. Runner is running on the next pitch. The batter hits a ground ball back toward the pitcher. The pitcher deflects the ball in the direction of the second baseman who defi-nitely has a chance to make a play on it. However, the ball strikes the runner before it reaches the second baseman.

   Ruling: Runner from first is **not** out; the ball remains alive and in play (assuming no intentional interference by the runner). (Com-pare with Play 5 on page 42.)

4. Bases loaded, no out. The infield is playing in. The batter hits a sharp ground ball which the third baseman deflects in the direction of the shortstop. Runner from second, seeing that the shortstop definitely will have a good chance of making a play on the ball, allows it to strike him. The ball caroms into left field and all runners take off.

   Ruling: Runner from second is guilty of intentionally interfering with a batted ball to break up a possible double play. Runner from second is out and so is the batter-runner. Runners return to first and third. Runner from second was guilty of violating Official Rule 7.09(g).

5. Runner on third, no out. Batter hits sharp ground ball down third base line which strikes runner on third base in fair territory while runner is still in contact with third base. Runner was not attempt-ing to intentionally interfere, and third baseman is playing behind the runner.

   Ruling: Runner is declared out. Ball is dead, and batter-runner is awarded first base. The fact that the runner had contact with the base when struck with the batted ball has no bearing on the play. (An exception to this is when the runner is hit by an infield fly while on base. See Section 4.7.)

6. Runner on second base, no one out. Batter bunts the ball down the third base line. Pitcher and third baseman hover over the ball and let it roll down the line toward third, hoping it will go foul. The ball continues to roll down the line in fair territory with the pitcher and third baseman following it. The ball ends up rolling to third base, strikes the base, and then strikes the runner from second base who is now standing on third.

Ruling: Even though the ball has technically not passed a fielder, the ball is alive and in play because the fielders had an opportunity to field the batted ball but chose not to. The runner is *not* out in this situation.

4.6 RUNNER INTERFERES WITH FIELDER WHILE IN CONTACT WITH BASE

If a runner has contact with a legally occupied base when he hinders a fielder attempting to make a play on a batted ball, he shall not be called out unless, in the umpire's judgment, such hindrance, whether it occurs on fair or foul territory, is intentional. If the umpire declares the hindrance **intentional**, the following penalty shall apply: With less than two out, the umpire shall declare both the runner and batter out. With two out, the umpire shall declare the batter out.

4.7 INFIELD FLY HITS RUNNER ON BASE

If a runner is touching his base when touched by an infield fly, he is not out, although the batter is out. Further, if the infield fly touches him while on base in fair territory before touching or passing an infielder, the ball is dead and no runners may advance.

4.8 INFIELD FLY HITS RUNNER NOT ON BASE

If a runner is touched by an infield fly when he is not touching his base, both runner and batter are out.

4.9 INFIELD FLY INTENTIONALLY DROPPED

If on an infield fly rule the infielder intentionally drops a fair ball, the ball remains **in play** despite the provisions of Official Rule 6.05(L). The infield fly rule takes precedence.

4.10 CATCHER INTERFERES WITH BATTER BEFORE PITCH

If the catcher interferes with the batter before the pitcher delivers the ball, it shall not be considered interference under Official Rule 6.08(c). In such cases, the umpire shall call "Time," and the pitcher and batter start over from "scratch."

4.11 BACKSWING HITS CATCHER

If a batter strikes at a ball and misses and swings so hard that he carries the bat all the way around and, in the umpire's judgment, unintentionally hits the catcher or the ball in back of him on the backswing (i.e., the follow-through), it shall be called a strike only (no interference). The ball will be dead, however, and no runner shall advance on the play. If this infraction should occur in a situation where the catcher's initial throw directly retires a runner despite the infraction, the play stands the same as if no violation had occurred. If this infraction should occur in a situation where the batter would normally become a runner because of a third strike not caught, the ball shall be dead and the batter declared out.

The proper mechanic is for the plate umpire to call, "Backswing hit the catcher!" as soon as the violation occurs (while pointing at the infraction), and then to call "Time" as the play dictates.

After the play is over, the umpire should then turn toward the press box and announce and signal that such infraction has occurred-the same as he should do with any unusual play-in order that the ruling be made as clear as possible.

4.12 BATTER INTERFERES WITH CATCHER'S THROW BACK TO PITCHER

If the batter interferes with the catcher's throw back to the pitcher by stepping out of the batter's box while he is at bat (no runners attempting to advance), it shall not be considered interference under Official Rule 6.06(c). In such cases, the umpire shall call "Time" only (no interference). The ball will be dead and no runner shall advance on the play.

This interpretation does not, of course, give the batter license to intentionally interfere with the catcher's throw back to the pitcher, and in such cases the batter shall be called out. If the batter becomes a runner on ball four and the catcher's throw strikes him or his bat, the ball remains alive and in play (provided no intentional interference by the batter-runner).

If the batter interferes with the catcher's throw to retire a runner by stepping out of the batter's box, interference shall be called on the batter under Official Rule 6.06(c).

However, if the batter is standing in the batter's box and he or his bat is struck by the catcher's throw back to the pitcher (or throw in attempting to retire a runner) and, in the umpire's judgment, there is no intent on the part of the batter to interfere with the throw, consider the ball alive and in play.

4.13 BATTER-RUNNER AND CATCHER COLLIDE

When a catcher and batter-runner going to first base have contact while the catcher is attempting to field the ball, there is generally no violation and nothing should be called. This cannot be interpreted to mean, however, that flagrant contact by either party would not call for either an interference call or an obstruction call. Either one should be called only if the violation is flagrant in nature. A fielder has "right of way" to make a play, but an unavoidable collision cannot be construed as a violation on the part of either the runner or the catcher.

4.14 THREE-FOOT LANE

The lines marking the three-foot lane are part of that "lane," but the interpretation to be made is that a runner is required to have **both feet** within the three-foot lane or on the lines marking the lane. If the runner straddles either boundary line running the last 45 feet to first base, he is outside the lane.

4.15 THROWN BAT INTERFERES WITH FIELDER

If a whole bat is thrown into fair territory and interferes with a defensive player attempting to make a play, interference shall be called, whether intentional or not. However, if a bat breaks and part of it is in fair territory and is hit by a batted ball or part of it hits a runner or fielder, play shall continue and no interference shall be called.

4.16 BATTED BALL STRIKES HELMET OR BAT

If a batted ball strikes a **helmet** accidentally (no intent on part of runner to interfere) in **fair** territory, the ball remains in play the same as if it had not hit the helmet.

If a batted ball strikes a **helmet** accidentally (no intent on part of runner to interfere) in **foul** territory, it is a foul ball.

If a batted ball strikes a **bat** or part of a bat accidentally (no intent on part of runner to interfere) in **foul** territory, it is a foul ball.

If the batter-runner drops his **bat** and the ball rolls against the bat in **fair** territory and, in the umpire's judgment, there was no intention to interfere with the course of the ball, the ball is alive and in play.

If after hitting or bunting a fair ball, the batter's **bat** hits the ball a second time in fair territory, the batter is out and the ball is dead.

If, in the umpire's judgment, there is intent on the part of a base runner to interfere with a batted ball (**fair or foul**) by dropping his helmet or bat or by throwing either at the ball, then the runner would be out, the ball dead, and runners would return to last base legally touched.

4.17 BATTED BALL STRIKES OBJECT ON FOUL TERRITORY

If a batted ball strikes a batting helmet or any other object foreign to the natural ground while on foul territory, it is a foul ball. (See exception in Section 4.19.)

4.18 THROWN BALL STRIKES HELMET OR BAT

If a thrown ball strikes a helmet or bat accidentally (no intent on part of runner to interfere) in fair or foul territory, the ball remains in play the same as if it had not hit the helmet or bat.

If, in the umpire's judgment, there is intent on the part of a base runner to interfere with a thrown ball by dropping his helmet or bat or by throwing either at the ball, then the runner would be out, the ball dead, and runners would return to the last base legally touched.

4.19 BALL STRIKES BIRD OR ANIMAL

If a batted or thrown ball strikes a bird in flight or other animal on the playing field, consider the ball alive and in play the same as if it had not touched the bird or animal.

4.20 INFIELDER INTERFERES WITH COURSE OF BALL

When a batted ball is rolling fair down the foul line between home plate and either first or third base and a fielder stoops down over the ball and blows on it or in any other manner does some act that in the judgment of the umpire causes the ball to roll onto foul territory, the umpire shall rule a fair ball.

4.21 OBSTRUCTION

Obstruction is the act of a fielder who, while not in possession of the ball and not in the act of fielding the ball, impedes the progress of any runner.

If a fielder is about to receive a thrown ball and if the ball is in flight directly toward and near enough to the fielder so he must occupy his position to receive the ball, he may be considered "in the act of fielding a ball." It is entirely up to the judgment of the umpire as to whether a fielder is in the act of fielding a ball.

After a fielder has made an attempt to field a ball and has missed, he can no longer be in the "act of fielding" the ball. For example: if an infielder dives at a ground ball and the ball passes him and he continues to lie on the ground and delays the progress of the runner, he very likely has obstructed the runner.

In all cases of obstruction, the umpire calling the play should have the benefit of the advice of his partners. The umpire watching the obstruction will have difficulty in determining the position of other runners. It is recommended that when "Time" is called on obstruction, if there is any doubt in the minds of the umpires about where the runner or runners shall be placed, the umpires shall confer.

4.22 OBSTRUCTION MECHANIC

There are two types of obstruction, and a different mechanic is used with each type.

(1) The first type of obstruction (Official Rule 7.06(a)) deals with cases when **the runner is obstructed _while_ a play is being made on him**. Examples of this type of obstruction include:

1. Runner is obstructed during a rundown.

2. Runner is obstructed as a fielder is making a direct throw to a base in an attempt to retire that runner.

3. Batter-runner is obstructed before reaching first base on a **ground ball to an infielder**.

4. Any other example where a play is being made directly on the runner at the moment he is obstructed.

This type of obstruction is to be signaled by the umpire immediately calling "Time" (both hands overhead) and then pointing laterally at the obstruction while calling loudly and clearly, "That's obstruction." The ball is dead immediately under this section of the obstruction rule, and all runners shall be awarded bases they would have reached had there been no obstruction. Furthermore, the obstructed runner shall be awarded at least one base beyond his last legally touched base at the time of obstruction.

Note that this section of the obstruction rule (i.e., runner obstructed while play being made on him) also provides for cases when a thrown ball is in flight at the moment the obstruction occurs. In such cases, the umpire shall take into consideration the results of the throw when making the award. As an example, if a throw is in flight at the moment the obstruction occurs (umpire calls "Time") and if the throw turns out to be wild and goes out of play, all runners will be awarded **two bases**. In such cases as this, the umpires have the responsibility of determining whether a throw is made **before** or **after** the obstruction. If the umpire judges that a throw was made after the obstruction, the obstructed runner will be awarded only **one base** from the base he last touched at the time of obstruction.

(2) The second type of obstruction (Official Rule 7.06(b)) deals with cases when **the runner is obstructed while _no play is being made on him_**. Examples of this type of obstruction include:

1. Batter-runner is obstructed in rounding first base on a base hit while ball is in the outfield.

38

2. Batter-runner is obstructed before reaching first base on a ball hit to the outfield.

3. Runner from first steals second; catcher's throw is wild and goes into center field; runner is obstructed in attempting to advance to third base. Ball is loose in outfield when obstruction occurs.

4. Runner from second is obstructed while rounding third base on a hit to the outfield.

5. Any other example where no play is being made directly on the runner at the moment he is obstructed.

Under this section of the obstruction rule, the obstruction is to be signaled by the umpire pointing laterally at the obstruction while calling loudly and clearly, "That's obstruction." The ball is **not** dead, however, and the umpire shall allow play to *continue until all play has ceased and no further action is possible*. At that moment, he shall call "Time" and impose such penalties, if any, that in his judgment will nullify the act of obstruction. It is important to note that in cases occurring under this section of the obstruction rule, the umpire shall not call "Time" until all action has ceased and no further play is possible.

Umpires are reminded that if a runner is obstructed under this second section of the obstruction rule, play is to proceed to completion—even if it results in a play later being made on the runner who was previously obstructed. However, if such a play on a previously obstructed runner results in that runner actually being tagged **out** before reaching the base to which he would have been awarded because of the obstruction, the umpire shall in that case call "Time" at the moment the runner is **tagged out**. He shall then impose such penalties that will nullify the obstruction which will include, of course, the obstructed runner being awarded the base to which he would be entitled because of the obstruction.

NOTE—*Runner Obstructed While No Play Being Made on Him*: In determining what base a runner will be awarded under this second section of the obstruction rule, it is permissible for the umpire to consider the position of the runner, ball, and fielder at the moment the obstruction occurs. However, the ultimate decision in placing the runners shall not be made until all play has ceased and shall be based on the principle that the obstructed runner will be entitled to the base he would have reached had no obstruction occurred.

The following play serves as an example:

Play: Batter-runner hits a fair ball down the right field line and is obstructed in rounding first base. At the moment the obstruction occurs, right fielder has not yet fielded the ball, and it appears at that moment that the batter-runner will end up with a stand-up double. However, as play proceeds, ball gets by the right fielder, and batter-runner continues on to third. Batter-runner is then thrown out at third base on a very close play.

Ruling: Since it is permissible for the umpire to consider the position of the runner, ball, and fielder at the moment the obstruction occurs, the umpire may initially plan on "protecting" the batter-runner as far as second base. However, as play continued, it became apparent that had the batter-runner not been obstructed in rounding first base, he would have reached third safely. Therefore, the moment the batter-runner is tagged out at third base, "Time" is called and batter-runner is awarded third on the obstruction. This decision is made on the principle that the umpire, in making awards on this type of obstruction, shall allow play to continue until no further action is possible and then shall make awards—if any—that will nullify the obstruction. In this example, if the umpire felt that the obstruction had no bearing on the fact that the batter-runner was thrown out at third, the out would stand.

4.23 BATTER-RUNNER OBSTRUCTED BEFORE REACHING FIRST BASE

When the batter-runner is obstructed before reaching first base, it is not always the case that the batter-runner will be awarded first base on this type of obstruction. For example, if the batter-runner is obstructed before reaching first base on a fly ball or line drive that is **caught**, the batter-runner is **out**. The reasoning here is that the obstruction had no bearing on the fact that the batter hit a fly ball that was caught by the defense. Similarly, should the batter-runner be obstructed before reaching first base on a **foul ball** not caught, the **foul ball** prevails. Again, the reasoning is that the obstruction had nothing to do with the fact that the batter hit a foul ball.

Situations where the batter-runner is obstructed before reaching first base can generally be divided into three cases. Again note that in this type of obstruction, it is *not* always the case that "Time" is called immediately and the batter-runner awarded first base.

Case 1: Batter-runner is obstructed before reaching first base on a ground ball to an infielder. It appears that the infielder will have an easy play on the ball.

Ruling: This is obstruction under Official Rule 7.06(a). "Time" is called immediately and batter-runner is awarded first base.

Case 2: Batter-runner is obstructed before reaching first base on a pop-up or line drive to an infielder.

Ruling: Call the obstruction by pointing at the obstruction and calling, "That's obstruction." However, leave the ball in play. If the pop-up or line drive is caught, batter-runner is out. **However**, if the pop-up or line drive is **dropped** (and is a fair ball) **and** if the batter-runner has not yet reached first base when the ball is dropped, "Time" is called and the batter-runner is awarded first base under Official Rule 7.06(a). Other runners would be awarded bases they would have reached had no obstruction occurred. (In this case, the play reverts back to Case 1 above.) On the other hand, if the batter-runner has clearly reached (or rounded) first base when the fly ball is dropped, play is allowed to continue until no further action is possible with the umpire then making awards—if any—that will nullify the obstruction. (In this case, the obstruction is treated as "Type 2" obstruction. See Section 4.22.)

Case 3: Batter-runner is obstructed before reaching first base on a ball hit to the outfield.

Ruling: Call the obstruction by pointing at the obstruction and calling, "That's obstruction"; however, leave the ball in play until all action has ceased. Then call "Time" and impose such penalties, if any, that will nullify the act of obstruction. If a fly ball is caught in this situation, batter-runner is out. If the batted ball was a fair ball not caught, the batter-runner will always be "protected" at least to first base.

4.24 OBSTRUCTION AND INTERFERENCE PLAYS—APPROVED RULINGS

1. Runner on first base; batter-runner gets in rundown between home and first. Can obstruction be called going back to home?

   Ruling: No, unless the obstruction is **intentional**.

   NOTE: In situations where the batter-runner gets in a rundown between first and home, if the batter-runner retreats and **reaches** home plate, he shall be declared out.

2. Batter-runner is obstructed before reaching first base with no play being made on him, for example, on a ball hit to the outfield.

   Ruling: Call the obstruction by pointing at the infraction and calling, "That's obstruction"; however, leave the ball in play until play is over. Then impose such penalties, if any, that will nullify the act of obstruction. If fly ball is caught in this situation, batter-runner is out.

3. Runner is on second base when batter-runner is obstructed after reaching first base. The umpire intends to award the batter-runner second base on the obstruction. What happens to the runner on second?

    Ruling: Runner on second is awarded third base.

4. With bases loaded, batter hits a sharp ground ball which deflects off of shortstop and starts to roll away from him. As shortstop starts to go after the ball, runner from second collides with him.

    Ruling: After the ball deflects off the shortstop, if the ball *is within the fielder's immediate reach*, the runner must avoid the fielder, and if contact occurs under those circumstances, **interference** shall be called and the runner declared out. However, if the ball is *not* within reach of the fielder after it deflects off him (i.e., the fielder must chase after the ball), the fielder must then avoid the runner, and if contact occurs under those circumstances, **obstruction** shall be called under Official Rule 7.06(b).

5. With a runner on first base, the batter hits a line drive back to the pitcher which deflects off of his glove and rolls toward the second baseman. As the second baseman is attempting to field the ball, the runner from first collides with the second baseman.

    Ruling: In the judgment of the umpire if the second baseman has a legitimate play on the ball, the runner from first is called out for interference. The ball is dead at the moment of interference, and the batter-runner is awarded first base (provided the interference was not intentional; if intentional, both runner and batter-runner are declared out). However, if the umpire rules that the second baseman does not have a legitimate play on the ball (i.e., he was merely moving in the direction of a loose ball), then obstruction is called under Official Rule 7.06(b). (Compare with Play 3 on page 33.)

6. Runner on first base, no one out. On a hit and run play, batter hits a fair ball down the right field line. In rounding second base and heading for third, the runner from first collides with the shortstop and falls down. Because of the collision, the runner is not able to advance to third base and returns to second as the ball is being thrown back to the infield. Had the runner not collided with the shortstop, he would have easily advanced to third base.

    Ruling: Obstruction is called when the collision occurs but the ball remains in play since no play was being made on the obstructed runner at the moment he was obstructed. "Time" is called when all action has ceased, and the obstructed runner is awarded third base since that is the base he would have reached had no obstruction occurred. Batter-runner would also be placed at the base he would have reached had no obstruction occurred (either first or second, depending on the umpire's judgment).

NOTE: In this play if the runner from first had been thrown out going back into second base, the umpire would call "Time" the moment the runner is tagged out. The obstructed runner would then be awarded third base (the base he would have reached had no obstruction occurred), and batter-runner would also be placed at the base he would have reached, in the umpire's judgment, had no obstruction occurred.

7. Batter hits a ground ball or pop-up between home and first base which the pitcher and first baseman both attempt to field. Batter-runner makes contact with one or both fielders in running to first base.

Ruling: Under Official Rule 7.09(L), *if two or more fielders attempt to field a batted ball and the runner comes in contact with one or more of them, the umpire shall determine which fielder is entitled to the benefit of the interference rule, and shall NOT declare the runner out for coming in contact with a fielder other than the one the umpire determines to be entitled to field such a ball.* It is therefore possible for the umpire to make either an **interference** or **obstruction** call on this play based upon his determination as to which fielder was entitled to field the batted ball. If the runner makes contact with a fielder other than the one the umpire determines to be entitled to field the ball, such a fielder has very likely obstructed the runner.

SECTION 5

PROGRESS OF THE GAME

5.1 TURNING ON LIGHTS

The umpire-in-chief shall order the playing field lights turned on whenever in his opinion darkness makes further play in daylight hazardous.

After a game has been started, the umpire-in-chief is to be the sole judge as to when field lights are to be turned on. He should call for the lights before the **beginning** of a full inning unless some extraordinary condition or abnormally long inning prompts otherwise. Umpires are instructed to use good judgment when asking for the lights. Umpires are to signal to turn off the lights when they are no longer needed during day games.

5.2 BETWEEN GAMES OF A DOUBLEHEADER

The second game of a doubleheader shall start twenty minutes after the first game is completed unless a longer interval is declared by the umpire-in-chief and announced to the opposing managers at the end of the first game.

The umpire-in-chief of the first game is the timekeeper and sole judge as to whether or not the second game is to start. The home club manager or management has no jurisdiction in determining this. **At the conclusion of the first game, the umpire-in-chief shall advise both managers of the exact starting time of the second game.**

Between games of a doubleheader, the umpire-in-chief shall have control of the groundskeeper and assistants for the purpose of making or keeping the playing field fit for play.

5.3 RAIN SITUATIONS

The umpire-in-chief shall be the sole judge as to whether and when play shall be suspended during a game because of unsuitable weather conditions or the unfit condition of the playing field; as to whether and when play shall be resumed after such suspension; and as to whether and when a game shall be terminated after such suspension. He shall not call the game until at least thirty minutes after he has suspended play. He may continue the suspension as long as he believes there is any chance to resume play.

The umpire-in-chief shall at all times try to complete a game. His authority to resume play following one or more suspensions of as much as thirty minutes each shall be absolute, and he shall terminate a game only when there appears to be no possibility of completing it.

The umpire crew chief should check weather bureau forecasts when rain is likely. When a game starts under threatening weather conditions, the umpire-in-chief should contact the groundskeeper and advise him to have his crew in readiness to handle field covers and drying materials. As soon as the umpire-in-chief receives the lineup cards, he shall become the sole judge as to whether a game is to continue or not. After time has been called because of weather conditions, Official Rule 3.10(c) authorizes the umpire to terminate the game after a wait of **at least thirty minutes**; but if in his judgment there is any chance to resume play, he may continue such suspension as long as his judgment warrants. In rain situations, **it is essential that umpires work with the executive-in-charge**, as the home club goes to great expense and obligation for each opening.

Between games of a doubleheader or whenever a game is suspended because of the unfitness of the playing field, the umpire-in-chief shall have control of the groundskeeper and assistants for the purpose of making the playing field fit for play.

During a rain delay, keep the following points in mind:

1. During the suspension of play, the crew chief and umpire-in-chief shall remain on one of the club's benches to observe the conditions and see that the playing field is tended to properly.

2. In games when weather is threatening one member of the crew should carry a watch. That umpire should note the time immediately when play is suspended.

3. Keep in communication with the general manager and/or the groundskeeper during the delay concerning weather developments.

4. The decision to terminate a game shall be made on the field and not in the dressing room.

A game should not be called without the crew chief finding out some of the problems that confront the club and to make sure the home club is prepared for cancellation. Before an umpire calls a game, he is to discuss the matter with the executive-in-charge. Also, before calling a game, the umpires are to consult within view of the stands. The consultation adds support to the decision.

If there is a second or subsequent delay in the same game, the umpires must wait at least thirty minutes after any such delay before calling the game.

5.4 CURFEWS AND TIME LIMITS

In making a decision as to when to invoke a curfew or time limit, the umpire shall rule that an inning or half-inning starts immediately after the third out is made in the preceding inning.

5.5 SUSPENDED GAMES

If a league adopts the optional suspended game rule (Official Rules 4.11(d) (3) through (6)), see Section 5.7. If a league has NOT adopted these rules, the following regulations shall apply regarding suspended games:

1. If a game is terminated because of **light failure, mechanical malfunction**, or **darkness**, it shall be a suspended game at any time after it starts.

2. If a game is terminated because of a **curfew** or **time limit**, it shall be a suspended game only if it has progressed far enough to be a regulation game under Official Rule 4.10. If such game has not progressed far enough to be a regulation game, it shall be declared **no game** and must be replayed in its entirety.

3. If a game is terminated because of **weather** during an incompleted full inning, it shall be a suspended game (provided it has progressed far enough to be a regulation game under Official Rule 4.10) if during the incompleted inning:

   a. The visiting team has scored one or more runs to tie the score, and the home team has not scored; or,

   b. The visiting team has scored one or more runs to take the lead, and the home team has not tied the score or retaken the lead.

   If such game has not progressed far enough to be a regulation game, it shall be declared **no game** and must be replayed in its entirety.

4. If a game is called before it has become a regulation game, it is **no game** and must be replayed in its entirety (unless Official Rule 4.12(a) (3) or (4) causes it to be a suspended game). (See paragraph 1 above in this section.)

5. Any **regulation** game called due to weather with the score tied is a **tie game** and must be replayed in its entirety (unless Official Rule 4.12(a)(5)(i) causes it to be a suspended game). (See paragraph 3a above in this section.)

5.6 REGULATION GAMES; OTHER RELATED TERMS

Under Official Rule 4.10(c), if a game is called off, it is a **regulation game** if:

1. **five innings** have been completed; or

2. **four and a half innings** have been completed and the home team is ahead; or

3. the home team scores one or more runs in its half of the **fifth inning** to **tie** the score.

There are other terms that are sometimes used when talking about regulation games or suspended games. These include terms such as "official game," "postponed game," "complete game," etc. Definitions for these terms are given below to help in understanding regulation and suspended games:

official game	Same as regulation game. (See definition above.)
complete game	Same as regulation game. (See definition above.)
legal game	Same as regulation game. (See definition above.)
called game, called off, or called	A game in which for **ANY** reason the umpire-in-chief terminates play.
suspended game	A game which has been called off but will be resumed from the exact point of suspension and completed at a later date. (See Sections 5.5 and 5.7.)
postponed game	A game which has been called off and must be replayed in its entirety at a later date. This term can also refer to a game which is called off before the game is started (due to unfit playing conditions of the field, for example). The term is also sometimes *improperly* used to apply to a *suspended* game. For example: "Tonight's game has been *postponed* because of light failure and will be resumed tomorrow prior to the regularly scheduled game." It would be more correct for the person to say, "Tonight's game has been *suspended* because of light failure and will be resumed tomorrow prior to the regularly scheduled game."
no game	A game which has been called off and must be replayed in its entirety at a later date (usually because the game was called off before it became a regulation game).

5.7 OPTIONAL SUSPENDED GAME RULE

If a league adopts the optional suspended game rule, the following regulations shall apply:

1. **If a game is called off BEFORE it becomes a regulation game, it shall become a SUSPENDED game.** (See Section 5.6, "Regulation Games; Other Related Terms.")

2. **If a game is called off at any point with the score TIED, it shall become a SUSPENDED game.**

3. **If a game is called off because of LIGHT FAILURE (or DARKNESS or MECHANICAL MALFUNCTION), it shall become a SUSPENDED game at any time after it starts.** For example, if a game is called off in the eighth inning because of light failure, it shall become a SUSPENDED GAME and must be completed in accordance with paragraph 6 below. Similarly, if a game is called off in the second inning because of light failure, it would also be a suspended game.

4. **If a game is called off because of a CURFEW or TIME LIMIT, it shall become a SUSPENDED game at any time after it starts.**

5. **If a <u>regulation</u> game is called off because of WEATHER during an INCOMPLETED INNING, it shall become a SUSPENDED game <u>IF</u> during the incompleted inning *the visiting team has scored one or more runs to take the lead, and the home team has not tied the score or retaken the lead.*** (See Official Rules 4.12(a)(5)(ii) and 4.11(d)(2).)

6. In accordance with Official Rule 4.12(c), such a suspended game must be resumed and completed from the exact point of suspension as follows:
   (a) Immediately preceding the next scheduled **single game** between the two clubs on the same grounds; or
   (b) Immediately preceding the next scheduled doubleheader between the two clubs on the same grounds **if no single game remains on the schedule**; or
   (c) If the game was suspended on the last scheduled date between the two clubs in that city, transferred and played on the grounds of the opposing club:
      (i) immediately preceding the next scheduled single game, or
      (ii) immediately preceding the next scheduled doubleheader between the two clubs if no single game remains on the schedule.

7. If the suspended game was called off **before** it had become a regulation game, the regular game following the completion of the suspended game shall be a **seven-inning** game.

8. If the suspended game was called off **after** it had become a regulation game, the regular game following the completion of the suspended game shall be a **nine-inning** game.

9. **The optional suspended game rule DOES NOT APPLY to games that are rained out AFTER they have become a regulation game (UNLESS** the score is **tied** when the game is called off or unless Official Rule 4.12(a)(5)(ii) applies). For example, if a game is rained out during the sixth inning, it is an "official" game, and the final score would be the score at the time the game was called off UNLESS:
   (a) the score was **tied**, in which case it would become a suspended game under paragraph 2 above; or
   (b) the game falls under Official Rule 4.12(a)(5)(ii), in which case it would become a suspended game under paragraph 5 above.

10. If a suspended game has not been completed prior to the last scheduled game between two clubs during the championship season, it shall become a called game.

11. The optional suspended game rule shall NOT be in effect
   (a) during the last scheduled game between two clubs during the championship season; or
   (b) during league playoffs.

12. Under these regulations as well as under the Official Rules, there is no provision whatsoever regarding "reverting back to the last completed inning" when a game is called off.

Each year every league files with the National Association its intention or non-intention of using the optional suspended game rule. All umpires must make absolutely certain before the start of the season whether or not their league is using this rule. (See Section 7.25.)

EXAMPLES:

1. A game is rained out at the end of the third inning with the home team leading 3-2.

   Ruling *(using optional suspended game rule)***:** Since the game was rained out before it became a regulation game, the game becomes a **suspended** game and must be resumed at the exact point of suspension immediately preceding the next scheduled single game between the two clubs in the same city as provided under Official Rule 4.12(c). (See paragraph 6 above.) The regularly scheduled game following the completion of this suspended game would be a **seven-inning** game.

Ruling *(NOT using optional suspended game rule)*: Since the game was called off before it became a regulation game, the game is declared **no game** and must be replayed in its entirety at a later date.

2. At the end of the seventh inning a game is tied 2-2. The game is rained out after the eighth inning with the score still 2-2.

   Ruling *(using optional suspended game rule)*: Since the score was tied when the game was called off, the game becomes a **suspended** game. The game following the completion of this suspended game would be a nine-inning game.

   Ruling *(NOT using optional suspended game rule)*: This is a regulation game called off with the score tied. The game is declared a tie game and must be replayed in its entirety at a later date.

3. A game is rained out at the end of the sixth inning with the home team leading 3-2.

   Ruling *(using optional suspended game rule)*: Home team wins the game 3-2.

   Ruling *(NOT using optional suspended game rule)*: Home team wins the game 3-2.

4. At the end of the seventh inning the home team is leading 3-2. In the top of the eighth inning the visiting team scores two runs to make the score 4-3. The game is rained out during the bottom of the eighth inning with the score still 4-3 in favor of the visiting club.

   Ruling *(using optional suspended game rule)*: This is a suspended game under Official Rule 4.12(a)(5)(ii). (See paragraph 5 in this section.) When the suspended game is completed, the game following would be a nine-inning game.

   Ruling *(NOT using optional suspended game rule)*: Exactly the same as the above ruling.

5. At the end of the seventh inning the home team is leading 3-2. In the top of the eighth inning the visiting team scores one run to tie the score 3-3. The game is rained out during the bottom of the eighth inning with the score still tied 3-3.

   Ruling *(using optional suspended game rule)*: This is a suspended game for two reasons. First, the game was called off with the score tied. Under the optional suspended game rule (see paragraph 2 in this section), any game called off with the score tied is a suspended game. Second, this game is also a suspended game under Official Rule 4.12(a)(5)(i). When the suspended game is completed, the game following would be a nine-inning game.

Ruling *(NOT using optional suspended game rule)*: This is a suspended game under Official Rule 4.12(a)(5)(i). The game following the completion of this suspended game would be a nine-inning game.

6. At the end of the seventh inning the home team is leading 3-2. In the top of the eighth inning the visiting team scores two runs to make the score 4-3. In the bottom of the eighth inning the home team scores one run to tie the score 4-4. The game is rained out during the bottom of the eighth inning with the score still tied 4-4.

Ruling *(using optional suspended game rule)*: Since the score was tied when the game was called off, the game becomes a suspended game. The game following the completion of this suspended game would be a nine-inning game.

Ruling *(NOT using optional suspended game rule)*: This game is a regulation game called off with the score tied. Therefore, the game is declared a **tie game** and must be replayed in its entirety at a later date. (Note that this game does not fall under Official Rules 4.12(a)(5)(i) or (ii).)

7. At the end of the fourth inning the visiting team is leading 3-2. In the bottom of the fifth inning the home team scores one run to tie the score. Before the fifth inning can be completed, the game is rained out with the score tied 3-3.

Ruling *(using optional suspended game rule)*: Since the score was tied when the game was called off, the game becomes a suspended game. Note that this game **is** a regulation game under Official Rule 4.10(c)(3). (See Section 5.6, Item 3.) Therefore, the game following completion of this suspended game would be a nine-inning game.

Ruling *(NOT using optional suspended game rule)*: This is a regulation game which is called off with the score tied. Therefore, the game is declared a **tie game** and must be replayed in its entirety at a later date.

8. At the end of the fourth inning the visiting team is leading 3-2. In the bottom of the fifth inning the home team scores two runs to make the score 4-3. Before the fifth inning can be completed, the game is rained out.

Ruling *(using optional suspended game rule)*: Home team wins the game 4-3.

51

Ruling *(NOT using optional suspended game rule)*: Home team wins the game 4-3.

9. A game is called off because of light failure during the third inning with the home team leading 3-2.

   Ruling *(using optional suspended game rule)*: Since the game was called off because of light failure, the game becomes a suspended game under Official Rule 4.12(a)(3). (See paragraph 3 in this section.) The game following the completion of this suspended game would be a seven-inning game.

   Ruling *(NOT using optional suspended game rule)*: This is a suspended game under Official Rule 4.12(a)(3). The game following the completion of this suspended game would be a nine-inning game.

10. A game is called off because of light failure during the eighth inning with the home team leading 3-2.

    Ruling *(using optional suspended game rule)*: Since the game was called off because of light failure, the game becomes a suspended game under Official Rule 4.12(a)(3). (See paragraph 3 in this section.) The game following the completion of this suspended game would be a nine-inning game.

    Ruling *(NOT using optional suspended game rule)*: Exactly the same as above ruling.

11. At the end of the fourth inning the home team is leading 3-2. In the top of the fifth inning the visiting team scores two runs to make the score 4-3. The game is rained out during the bottom of the fifth inning with the score still 4-3 in favor of the visiting team.

    Ruling *(using optional suspended game rule)*: Since the game was called off before it became a regulation game, the game becomes a suspended game. The game following the completion of the suspended game would be a seven-inning game.

    Ruling *(NOT using optional suspended game rule)*: Since the game was called off before it became a regulation game, the game is declared **no game** and must be replayed in its entirety at a later date. (Note that Official Rule 4.12(a)(5)(ii) does not apply to this game because the game had not become a regulation game. See Official Rule 4.12(b).)

12. At the end of the fourth inning the home team is leading 3-2. In the top of the fifth inning the visiting team scores two runs to make the

score 4-3. In the bottom of the fifth inning the home team scores one run to tie the score 4-4. The game is rained out during the bottom of the fifth inning with the score tied 4-4.

Ruling *(using optional suspended game rule)*: Since the score was tied when the game was called off, the game becomes a suspended game. Under Official Rule 4.10(c)(3) (see Section 5.6, Item 3), this game **is** a regulation game. Therefore, the game following completion of this suspended game would be a nine-inning game.

Ruling *(NOT using optional suspended game rule)*: Because the home team tied the score in the bottom of the fifth inning, this is a regulation game. (See Section 5.6, Item 3.) Therefore, this is a regulation game called off with the score tied. The game is declared a **tie game** and must be replayed in its entirety at a later date.

13. At the end of the fourth inning the home team is leading 3-2. In the top of the fifth inning the visiting team scores one run to tie the score 3-3. The game is rained out in the bottom of the fifth inning with the score still tied 3-3.

    Ruling *(using optional suspended game rule)*: This is a suspended game for two reasons. First, the game was called off with the score tied. Second, the game was called off before it became a regulation game. The game following the completion of this suspended game would be a seven-inning game. (Note that Official Rule 4.12(a)(5)(i) does not apply here because the game was not a regulation game.)

    Ruling *(NOT using optional suspended game rule)*: Since the game was called off before it became a regulation game, the game is declared **no game** and must be replayed in its entirety at a later date.

14. At the end of the seventh inning a game is tied 3-3. In the top of the eighth inning the visiting team scores one run to make the score 4-3. The game is rained out in the bottom of the eighth inning with the score still 4-3.

    Ruling *(using optional suspended game rule)*: This is a suspended game under Official Rule 4.12(a)(5)(ii). (See paragraph 5 in this section.) The game following the completion of this suspended game would be a nine-inning game.

    Ruling *(NOT using optional suspended game rule)*: Exactly the same as the above ruling.

15. At the end of the seventh inning a game is tied 3-3. In the top of the eighth inning the visiting team scores one run to make the score 4-3. In the bottom of the eighth inning the home team scores one run to tie the score 4-4. The game is rained out before the eighth inning can be completed with the score still 4-4.

   Ruling (*using optional suspended game rule*)**:** Since the score was tied when the game was called off, the game becomes a suspended game. The game following the completion of this suspended game would be a nine-inning game.

   Ruling (*NOT using optional suspended game rule*)**:** This is a regulation game called off with the score tied. Therefore, the game is declared a **tie game** and must be replayed in its entirety at a later date. Note that Official Rule 4.12(a)(5)(ii) does not apply to this game because the home team tied the score in the bottom of the eighth inning.

5.8   WEATHER TAKING PRECEDENCE

Weather and similar conditions shall take precedence in determining whether a called game shall be a suspended game.

If play is stopped because of **weather** and during the delay (before the tarps have been removed) **a curfew or time limit** is reached, the game will be considered as having been terminated because of **weather** and shall not be a suspended game.

If play is stopped because of **weather** and during the delay (before the tarps have been removed) **light failure** occurs and causes the game to be terminated, the game will be considered as having been terminated because of **weather** and shall not be a suspended game.

However, in games that have been delayed because of **weather**, once the umpires direct the grounds crew to remove the tarps and prepare the field for play, **the weather factor is then removed**. In such cases, if light failure then occurs or if a curfew or time limit is subsequently reached, the game will be considered a **suspended** game.

If play is stopped because of **light failure** and rain subsequently occurs before play can be resumed, the umpires shall then determine the ultimate reason for terminating the game. Consider the following examples:

1. Game stopped because of light failure; rain occurs during light failure; lights come back on during or after rain; field determined to be unplayable.

   Ruling: Game called due to weather. Not a suspended game.

2. Game stopped because of light failure; rain occurs during light failure; field determined to be unplayable and still no lights.

Ruling: Game called due to weather. Not a suspended game.

3. Game stopped because of light failure; a light rain occurs during light failure; rain stops and field determined to be playable but still no lights.

Ruling: Game called because of light failure. This is a suspended game.

5.9 LINEUP CARDS FROM SUSPENDED GAMES

In a suspended game, the umpire-in-chief must make notation on the lineup cards of the exact situation the moment play is suspended. Included should be the following information: inning, score, outs, runners on base (by name), batter, count on the batter, and defensive player due to bat first the next inning. The same cards will be used when the suspended game is resumed.

In cases where the suspended game is the last game of a series, the lineup cards (with exact situation at moment of suspension outlined above) should be photocopied and photocopy retained by the original umpire crew. The original lineup cards and situation should be forwarded within twenty-four hours to the league office along with any other pertinent information.

5.10 PROTESTED GAMES

When a manager officially protests a game, claiming that an umpire's decision is in violation of the rules, he must announce the protest to the umpire-in-chief **before** the next pitch, play, or attempted play. A protest arising on a game-ending play may be filed until 12 noon the following day with the league office.

If a manager officially protests a game, **all** the umpires shall confer and discuss the play or situation on which the protest is lodged. It must be determined by the crew that the umpire making the call has made a proper ruling. If the crew is certain the ruling was correct as made, the umpire-in-chief shall accept the manager's protest and have the P.A. announcer announce that the game is being played under protest. The opposing manager is to be informed that the game is being played under protest.

In accepting the protest, the umpires shall:

1. Ascertain the manager's exact reason or grounds for protest. This must be done before the protest can be accepted.

2. Confer as a crew, making certain their ruling is correct.

3. Have the protest announced over the P.A. system.

4. Make notation on the lineup cards as to the exact situation at moment of protest (inning, score, outs, runners on base, batter, count on the batter, and defensive player due to bat first the next inning).

The umpires shall report by telephone the next morning to the league office that the game was protested and the reason for the protest. A detailed written report shall be sent to the league office within twenty-four hours. The lineup cards (with exact situation at moment of protest) should be photocopied and photocopy retained by the umpire crew. The original lineup cards and situation should be forwarded to the league office with the written report.

All umpires of the crew shall sign the report on a protested game.

5.11 RIGHT TO POSTPONE

The management of the home team shall be the sole judge as to whether a game shall not be started because of unsuitable weather conditions or the unfit condition of the playing field except for the second game of a double-header.

Note, however, that some leagues have a provision for transferring the responsibility of postponement to the umpires when clubs meet for the final time during the season. For example, certain leagues give the umpires sole responsibility for postponing the start of a game during the last series between two clubs in either city. Other leagues give the umpires this responsibility only for the very last series in which the clubs meet. Other leagues have no provision for this whatsoever. In any case, it is **essential** that the umpires always work closely with the general manager in such games.

Make certain that you are thoroughly familiar with the manner in which your league president wants you to handle these situations.

5.12 LINEUPS AND POSTPONED/SUSPENDED GAMES

Should a game be called off after the lineup cards have been turned in to the umpire-in-chief but before the umpire has called "Play" to start the game, such game would be considered as having been postponed prior to starting and not be a suspended game (since the game has not officially started). The tender of the home team's batting order to the umpire-in-chief conveys control of the playing field to the umpires; this does not represent the start of the game. The game does not begin until the umpire calls "Play" to start the game. Managers would not be held to their original lineups when a game is rescheduled under such a postponement.

If a game becomes suspended during a manager's or coach's trip to the mound (or after the trip but while the same batter is still at bat), a new pitcher may be substituted when the game is later resumed.

If a rain delay occurs during a manager's or coach's trip to the mound (or after the trip but while the same batter is still at bat), a new pitcher may be substituted when the game is resumed following the rain delay.

If immediately prior to a game becoming suspended, a substitute pitcher has been announced but has not retired the side or pitched until the batter has become a runner, such a pitcher may, but is not required to, start the resumed portion of the game. If he does not start when the game is resumed, he will be considered as having been substituted for and may not be used in that game.

5.13 TEMPORARY FAILURE OF LIGHTS

This regulation is provided as a clarification and further explanation of Official Rule 5.10(b) (i.e., in situations when light failure makes it difficult or impossible for umpires to follow the play):

In the event of a temporary failure of lights while a ball is in flight or a play is in progress and the umpires are not able to follow the play because of the light failure, the umpire will immediately call "Time." When the lights are turned on again and play is resumed, the batter and all runners shall return to the last base touched by them at the time of suspension. If the batter has not reached first base at the time of suspension, he shall return to the batter's box and assume the same count of balls and strikes he had at the time of suspension.

In the event of inability to complete a double play because of failure of lights, a decision will be rendered only on that part of the play completed before time was called for light failure.

Under Official Rule 5.10(b), individual leagues may also adopt their own regulations regarding light failure. The following examples serve as sample U.D.P. interpretations:

EXAMPLES:

1. With runner(s) on base, batter hits a deep fly ball to the outfield. It is possible that the fly ball may become a home run. Light failure occurs while the ball is still in the air.

    Ruling: All runners return and batter returns to bat with the same ball and strike count before the light failure.

2. With runner on first base, batter hits a ground ball to shortstop. The out is made at second base, but total light failure occurs as the ball is about to be thrown to first base.

    Ruling: Out at second base stands. Batter returns to bat with same ball and strike count before the light failure.

3. With runner(s) on base, batter hits a deep fly ball to the outfield which is ruled a home run. Light failure occurs before the batter-runner reaches first base.

    Ruling: The home run is allowed. When play resumes, the batter and all runners resume their places at the time of the light failure and are allowed to touch bases in accordance with base-running rules.

SECTION 6

PITCHING REGULATIONS

6.1   WINDUP POSITION

If a pitcher holds the ball with both hands in front of his body, with his entire pivot foot on or in front of and touching but not off the end of the pitcher's plate and his other foot free, he will be considered in a windup position. From this position he may:

1. Deliver the ball to the batter, or

2. Step and throw to a base in an attempt to pick off a runner, or

3. Disengage the rubber (if he does he must drop his hands to his sides).

In disengaging the rubber, the pitcher must step off with his pivot foot and not his free foot first.

From the windup position the pitcher may not go into a set or stretch position—if he does, it is a balk.

Note that some pitchers assume their windup position with their hands **apart** (arms at their sides) and then go directly into their delivery to the plate from this position. Other pitchers assume their windup position with their hands apart and then bring their hands together and come to a stop before beginning their delivery to the plate. Either of these two positions is considered a legal windup position, and from either windup position (regardless of whether the pitcher's hands are together or apart), the pitcher may:

1. Deliver the ball to the batter, or

2. Step and throw to a base in an attempt to pick off a runner, or

3. Disengage the rubber by stepping off with his pivot foot first. (Disengaging the rubber by stepping back with his free foot first is a balk when runners are on base regardless of whether the pitcher's hands are together or apart.)

6.2   INTENTIONALLY PITCHING AT THE BATTER

The following regulations are a result of the of the provisions of the On-Field Behavior Policy (see Section 7.29) and supersede the directives in Official Playing Rule 8.02(d).

A pitcher judged by the plate umpire to have intentionally delivered a pitched ball at a batter <u>will be immediately ejected</u> from the game. No warning will be given. (Note that the umpire does not have the three options given in Official Playing Rule 8.02(d) in dealing with this infraction.)

If the league president deems that the act was intentional, this infraction carries an automatic fine and suspension as provided in the On-Field Behavior Policy (see Section 7.29).

At the time of the ejection, the umpire shall <u>warn the manager of both teams</u> that another such pitch by any pitcher during the game will result in the immediate expulsion of the pitcher <u>and</u> that pitcher's manager.

If, in the umpire's judgment, circumstances warrant, an official "warning" may be issued to both clubs prior to the start of the game or at any time during the game. (Note that the "warning" would take the form of a "reminder" to all parties that under the On-Field Behavior Policy, the penalty for intentionally throwing at a batter is *immediate* ejection from the game.)

(See Section 7.29, "On-Field Behavior Policy.")

6.3   PITCHER POSSESSING FOREIGN SUBSTANCE

The pitcher shall not have on his person or in his possession any foreign substance. For such infraction, the penalty shall be immediate ejection from the game.

The term "foreign substance" shall include any object, material, or substance that could, in the judgment of the umpires, be used to deface or "doctor" the ball in any manner.

In a situation in which the pitcher refuses to allow an umpire to inspect his equipment, uniform, or person when the umpire suspects a foreign substance, the pitcher shall be ejected from the game.

6.4   SPECIAL BALK REGULATIONS

(a) The pitcher shall be charged with a balk if he attempts a pick-off at first base and throws to the first baseman who is either in front of or behind first base and obviously not making an attempt at retiring the runner. However, there is no violation if the pitcher throws the ball directly to *first base* in this situation. Also note that there is no violation if the pitcher attempts a pick-off at second or third and throws to an infielder who is in front of or behind either of those bases (i.e., this violation is only in reference to pick-offs at *first base*).

(b) A right- or left-handed pitcher shall be committed to **pitch or throw to second base** when he swings his entire free foot completely behind the back edge of the rubber.

(c) The pitcher shall be charged with a balk if he stands **on or astride** the pitcher's plate without the ball. (He may be on the dirt without the ball.)

(d) A pitched ball which slips out of a pitcher's hand and crosses the foul line shall be called a ball; otherwise it will be called no pitch. If the ball does not cross the foul line, this would be a balk with men on base.

(e) The pitcher, while touching his plate, must step **directly** toward a base before throwing to that base. (See Section 6.5, "Stepping to a Base.") If a pitcher turns or spins off of his free foot without actually stepping or if he turns his body and throws before stepping, it is a balk.

(f) If a pitcher, while touching his plate, jumps into the air with both feet simultaneously and his non-pivot foot lands in a **step** toward first base before he throws to that base, he has made a legal move. (See Section 6.5, "Stepping to a Base.")

(g) If the pitcher places the resin bag in his glove with, in the umpire's judgment, the intent of deceiving the runner, it is a balk.

(h) If the pitcher steps off of the rubber with his non-pivot foot when pitching from the windup position, the pitcher shall be charged with a balk.

(i) It is legal for a right-handed pitcher to begin a pick-off move to first base by first moving his pivot foot in the direction of third base **provided** that he makes a legal **step** toward first base with his non-pivot foot before throwing there and provided that the move is continuous and without interruption. A pitcher who makes such a pick-off move is considered to be in contact with the rubber when he makes his throw to first base.

(j) It is a balk if the pitcher, after coming to a legal pitching position, removes one hand from the ball other than in an actual pitch or in throwing to a base.

(k) Prior to assuming a legal pitching position (windup or set position) it is permissible for the pitcher to **momentarily adjust** the ball in his glove. In order for this to be allowed, the movement must be **momentary** in nature. If the pitcher has his hands together long enough that, in the judgment of the umpire, it appears that he has actually come to a set position or has actually assumed the wind-up position, then should the pitcher separate his hands, a balk shall be called under Official Rule 8.05(j).

(l) There is no violation if a pitcher attempts a pick off at second base and seeing no fielder covering the bag, throws to the shortstop or second

60

baseman, neither of whom is in the vicinity of the bag nor is making an actual attempt to retire the runner.

(m) A pitcher who assumes his windup position with the <u>heel</u> of his non-pivot foot off the ground is to be charged with a balk if in stepping off the rubber he drops the heel of his non-pivot foot before disengaging the rubber with his pivot foot.

(n) With runners on first and third, if a pitcher fakes a throw to third base and then throws the ball to first base, *arm motion* is *not* required by the pitcher in his fake to third. (See Official Rule 8.05(c), second casebook ruling.)

6.5   STEPPING TO A BASE

The pitcher, while touching the rubber, must step **directly** toward a base before throwing to that base. If a pitcher turns or spins off of his free foot without actually stepping, it is a balk.

In stepping to a base, the pitcher must lift his entire non-pivot foot off the ground and bring it down in a location different from where it started and toward the base. The entire non-pivot foot must move in a **direction** toward and **distance** to the base. This will constitute a step. He is not allowed to lift his non-pivot foot up and bring it back down in the same spot where it started. In stepping, the heel of his free foot may not end up in the same spot it started.

6.6   THROWING TO AN UNOCCUPIED BASE

Official Rule 8.05(d) provides that the pitcher be charged with a balk if, while in contact with the rubber, he throws to an unoccupied base except for the purpose of making a play.

Play: Runners on first and second, pitcher in set position. Runner breaks for third base and pitcher throws to third base.

Ruling: Legal play.

Play: Runners on first and second, pitcher in set position. Runner bluffs going to third base and pitcher throws to third base. However, runner did not go.

Ruling: Balk under Official Rule 8.05(d).

The key to understanding the above two plays is for the umpire to use good judgment in deciding whether or not the runner was making an actual attempt to advance to third base or whether he was *bluffing*. These plays will most likely happen with a 3-2 count and 2 out.

Another interpretation regarding Official Rule 8.05(d) concerns appeal plays:

It is NOT a balk for the pitcher, while in contact with the rubber, to throw to an unoccupied base IF it is for the purpose of making an appeal play.

6.7 BALK MECHANIC

In calling a balk, the umpire shall point laterally at the pitcher and call loudly, "That's a balk." However, the ball is not dead automatically when this call is made. The ball becomes dead when the umpire calls "Time" following the call of balk, and the call of "Time" is to be made only when play stops. Note that the umpire's call of "Time" following the initial call of the balk is to be as **loud and emphatic** as the original call of balk.

The question arises as to when the umpire is to call "Time" to kill the ball after calling a balk. The following cases should help explain when play is considered *"stopped"* and at what moment the umpire should call "Time" following the call of balk:

1. If the pitcher balks and does not throw the ball, call "That's a balk; time" and enforce the balk.

2. If the balk is followed by a batted ball, leave the ball in play until it is apparent that the batter and all runners will not advance one base. At that moment, call "Time" and enforce the balk.

    > Example (1): If a batted ball follows the balk and results in a fly ball that is caught, call "Time" the moment the fly ball is caught. Then enforce the balk.

    > Example (2): If a batted ball follows the balk and results in a ground out on a previous runner at the base to which he would be entitled because of the balk, call "Time" the moment the out is made. Then enforce the balk.

    If, however, the batter reaches first and all runners advance at least one base on play following the balk, play proceeds **without reference to the balk**.

3. If the balk is followed by a pitch that is **caught** by the catcher, call "Time" the moment the catcher catches the ball. Then enforce the balk. (Note exception in ball four situations covered in case 5 below.)

4. If the balk is followed by a pick-off throw to a base that is **caught** by a fielder, call "Time" the moment the fielder catches the ball. Then enforce the balk.

5. If the balk is followed by ball four delivered to the batter and is caught by the catcher, call "Time" and enforce the balk *unless* all runners advance one base because of ball four. In that situation, play proceeds **without reference to the balk**.

6. If the balk is followed by a pitch which strikes the batter, call "Time" the moment the pitch strikes the batter. Then enforce the balk unless the hit batsman forces <u>all</u> other runners to advance one base, in which case play proceeds without reference to the balk.

7. If the balk is followed by a **wild throw** to a base, the Approved Ruling of Official Rule 8.05 provides that the runner may advance beyond the base to which he is entitled at his own risk. In that situation, the umpire shall call the balk in the usual manner but shall not call "Time" until *all play has ceased* (runners have stopped trying to advance **and** a fielder is in possession of the ball in the infield).

8. If the balk is followed by a **wild pitch**, the Approved Ruling of Official Rule 8.05 provides that the runner may advance beyond the base to which he is entitled at his own risk. In that situation, the umpire shall call the balk in the usual manner but shall not call "Time" until *all play has ceased* (runners have stopped trying to advance **and** a fielder is in possession of the ball in the infield).

Note that even if the runner advances to or beyond the base to which he is entitled because of a wild pitch following a balk, the balk is still "acknowledged." That is, the pitch is nullified and the batter will resume his at bat with the count on him when the balk occurred unless

(a) The wild pitch was ball four on which all runners advanced one base; or

(b) The wild pitch was strike three on which the batter and all other runners advanced one base.

In both situations (a) and (b) above, play proceeds **without reference to the balk**, since all runners (including the batter-runner) advanced one base on the pitch following the balk.

6.8 PENALTY FOR BALK

Under Official Rule 8.05, the penalty for a balk shall be: The ball is dead (**when play stops**), and each runner shall advance one base without liability to be put out unless the batter reaches first on a hit, an error, a base on balls, a hit batter, or otherwise and all other runners advance at least one base, in which case the play proceeds without reference to the balk.

Note that in cases where a pitcher balks and throws wild, either to a base or home plate, a runner or runners may advance beyond the base to which he is entitled at his own risk.

6.9   TRIPS TO THE MOUND BY MANAGER OR COACH

A second trip to the mound to the same pitcher in the same inning by a manager or coach will cause that pitcher's removal **from the game**.

The manager or coach is prohibited from making a second visit to the mound while the same batter is at bat, but if a pinch hitter is substituted for this batter, the manager or coach may then make a second visit to the mound but must remove the pitcher.

For the purpose of this rule, a batter's time at bat begins the moment the preceding batter is put out or becomes a base runner.

A manager or coach is considered to have concluded his visit to the mound when he leaves the 18-foot circle surrounding the pitcher's rubber. When the manager or coach leaves the 18-foot circle, he must keep going and not return to the mound.

One of the effects of the rule regarding trips to the mound is as follows: Once a manager or coach has made a trip to the mound, the pitcher then pitching must continue pitching to the batter then at bat (or retire the side) unless a pinch hitter is substituted or unless one of the following situations applies:

(a)   If a game becomes suspended during a manager's or coach's trip to the mound (or after the trip but while the same batter is still at bat), a new pitcher may be substituted when the game is later resumed.

(b)   If a rain delay occurs during a manager's or coach's trip to the mound (or after the trip but while the same batter is still at bat), a new pitcher may be substituted when the game is resumed following the rain delay.

If the catcher or any other player goes to the dugout and then immediately to the mound, it will be considered a visit to the mound by the manager.

If the manager or coach goes to the catcher or infielder and that player then goes to the mound (or the pitcher goes to the infielder at his position) before there is an intervening play (a pitch or other play), that will be the same as the manager or coach going to the mound.

If a pitcher is removed and the manager or coach remains to talk to the new pitcher, this is not charged as a visit with the new pitcher.

If the coach goes to the mound and removes a pitcher and then the manager goes to the mound to talk with the new pitcher, that will constitute one trip to that new pitcher that inning.

If a manager changes pitchers and leaves the mound, he (or a coach) *may* come out again to visit the pitcher *while the same batter is at bat*, but this will constitute one trip to that new pitcher that inning.

In a case where a manager has made his first trip to the mound and then attempts to return a second time to the mound in the same inning with the same batter at bat, he shall be **warned** by the umpire that he cannot return to the mound. If the manager ignores such warning, he shall be removed from the game and the pitcher required to pitch to the batter until he is retired or gets on base. After the batter is retired or becomes a base runner, then this pitcher must be removed from the game. The manager should be notified that his pitcher will be removed from the game after he pitches to one hitter so he can have a substitute pitcher warmed up. In this case, the substitute pitcher will be allowed eight preparatory pitches or more if in the umpire's judgment circumstances justify.

NOTE: If through umpire error, the manager is inadvertently allowed to go to the mound a second time while the same batter is at bat (**without** the manager being **warned** that he cannot do so), the pitcher then pitching will be required to pitch to the batter then at bat until he is retired or gets on base. After the batter is retired or becomes a base runner, this pitcher must then be removed from the game. **However**, because the umpire failed to **warn** the manager that he was not allowed to make a second trip to the mound while the same batter was at bat, the manager is **NOT** to be ejected from the game in this situation.

The manager may request permission from the umpire to visit the mound in case of injury to or illness of the pitcher, and with permission granted it will not be counted as a visit to the mound. The umpire-in-chief shall accompany the manager or coach in such situations and remain in the vicinity of the conference to ensure this regulation is not abused. The opposing manager is to be informed at the conclusion of the conference that this is not a visit.

6.10 TRIPS TO THE MOUND BY PLAYER-MANAGER

While playing, any visit to the mound by a player-manager will be considered a trip. The umpire shall notify the player-manager and the opposing manager each time a trip is charged.

6.11 TRIPS TO THE MOUND BY PLAYER-COACH

While playing, a player-coach will be treated as a player until he is considered to have abused the privilege. If, in the judgment of the umpire, the privilege is abused, the player-coach and his manager will be advised that any future visits to the mound will be charged as trips.

6.12 PITCHER CHANGING POSITIONS

A pitcher may change to another position only once during the same inning; i.e., the pitcher will not be allowed to assume a position other than a pitcher more than once in the same inning.

If a pitcher changes positions and then returns to the mound during the same inning, he will be allowed the usual eight warm-up pitches.

6.13 PITCHER EJECTED

If a pitcher is ejected during an inning in which he is pitching, the substitute pitcher should have time for a full warm-up similar to the time allowed when an injured pitcher is removed from the game.

6.14 AMBIDEXTROUS PITCHERS

In the rare occasion of an ambidextrous pitcher, the pitcher and batter may each change positions **one time** per at-bat. For example, if the pitcher changes from right-handed to left-handed and the batter then changes batter's boxes, each player must remain that way for the duration of that at-bat (unless the offensive team substitutes a pinch hitter, and then each player may again "switch" one time).

SECTION 7

INSTRUCTIONS TO UMPIRES

7.1 REPORTING TROUBLE

Anything that is not "routine" should be called in to the league office early the next morning or, at the discretion of the league president, the night of the game. Examples of this include fights, bumping incidents, bean ball incidents, protested games, etc. The identical report should then be mailed to the league office within twenty-four hours. Extreme care should be taken in preparing the report.

In cases of a violent nature (bumping, assault on an umpire, confrontation off the field, etc.), a copy of the umpire's report is also to be sent within twenty-four hours to the Baseball Office for Umpire Development.

7.2 UMPIRE REPORTS

In writing your reports, remember that they are actually legal documents and that others may be privileged to examine them. Tell precisely what happened and the exact language that was used. Be sure of your facts and confine your report to the facts only. Do not "editorialize." Give facts, and the situation will take care of itself. In fashioning the report, do not say a manager or player was "run" or "chased"; instead say, "removed" or "ejected."

Take extreme care in writing your reports. Make sure spelling and punctuation are correct. Always proofread the report to make sure it is free of errors and clear to the reader.

Always keep a copy of the report for your own records.

Any umpire report should be postmarked within twenty-four hours after the incident being reported.

7.3 NO VISITORS IN DRESSING ROOMS

No visitors shall be permitted at any time in the umpires' dressing rooms. The term "visitors" shall include club officers and employees, newspaper, radio, and television representatives, photographers, friends, and relatives. No one except the umpires, umpire supervisors, league officers, and the clubhouse attendant assigned to the umpires' room shall be permitted in these rooms before, during, or after a ball game. **There are no exceptions to this rule.** The umpire-in-chief shall be responsible for its enforcement and for reporting any violations to the league president.

67

The National Association has furnished each club with printed posters of the "NO ADMITTANCE" regulation. This regulation shall be posted outside the entrance to the umpires' dressing rooms and shall be strictly enforced.

7.4 COOPERATION WITH PRESS, RADIO, AND TELEVISION

Always cooperate with the news media when possible. Avoid arguments and refer any controversial matters to the league president. Coordinate with television personnel when games are televised.

Umpires should cooperate with press, radio, and television personnel in explaining controversial plays which occur in the game and events happening in a "rhubarb." In the discussion, umpires should realize they are not to suggest any action the league president might take after receiving the report of the incident.

In a protested game or a controversy over an interpretation of a playing rule or a ground rule which will be decided by the league president, the umpire should not prejudge the action the league president will take, and in these cases it would be better for the umpire to refer the matter to the league president. However, the umpire can certainly explain what actually happened on the field.

In situations where a manager, coach, or player is ejected from a game, all the umpire need do is tell the press, radio, or television personnel that the man was ejected for something he said, or for some gestures he used, or for violating the rule against arguing balls and strikes, etc.

Umpires are required to use judgment in answering various questions which the press, radio, and television personnel ask them. These people want further facts so they can write a more informative story for the fans. There is no restriction on the umpire commenting to the extent of relating the actual facts of the decision. In fact, such cooperation helps to get the matter properly before the fans through the press, radio, or television.

7.5 UPON ARRIVAL TO CITY

Upon arriving in a city to fulfill your assignment, the crew chief is to inform by telephone to the top executive operating the ball club of the crew's presence and check with him on the starting times of games in the series that are to be handled by the crew. The crew chief is also to inform the club of the telephone number where the crew may be reached while in that city. **Do not fail to do this.** Some afternoon games and doubleheaders are scheduled. Be sure you know all starting times.

7.6 ARRIVAL AT BALL PARK:

Umpires are to arrive at the ball park no later than one hour prior to the scheduled starting time of the game. The individual league president may specify an earlier arrival time.

Umpires are to dress in a professional manner to and from the park; dress slacks and shirts are recommended. Jeans or tennis shoes are not acceptable dress to and from the park. Socks shall be worn by all umpires.

Should a league specify that one of the umpires is to sit in the stands for a specified time prior to the start of the game for pre-game observation, that umpire should realize that this is an official duty and not a time for fraternization with fans or club employees. Nor is this a time for personal matters (reading a book, for example). Remember as just stated that this is an official duty.

Umpires are to stay out of club offices unless official business requires otherwise. Similarly, umpires should be cautious regarding casual fraternization with club employees. Each umpire has a duty to perform once at the ball park, and over-familiarity with club officials should not be one of them.

All umpires are to abide by the "No Admittance" rule posted outside each dressing room (see Section 7.3).

All umpires on the crew should be completely dressed and ready to take the field 15 minutes prior to the scheduled starting time should a sudden emergency arise.

7.7   BASEBALLS

The home club will deliver a supply of regulation baseballs to the umpires before the start of a game. The number and make of the baseballs will be certified by the league president. Umpires are to rub up all baseballs well. Certainly all baseballs delivered to the umpires before the game for rubbing should get into the baseball bag for the game. Baseballs are the single most costly item of playing equipment for a club. Every effort should be taken to get as much game use as possible before discarding as unfit, consistent with good standards of play, any baseball.

Theft of baseballs by an umpire will be grounds for immediate dismissal.

7.8   AT HOME PLATE BEFORE A GAME

All umpires assigned to work a game should walk together as a crew to the plate five minutes before the start of a game. In some parks where the national anthem is played after the players take their positions on the field, five minutes may not be sufficient. The crew chief should fix the time for arriving at the plate early enough to permit ground rules discussions to be completed so that the game starts (umpire calls "Play") within a few seconds of the official starting time. *Start games on time!*

7.9   GROUND RULES

Be very sure that you are thoroughly familiar with ground rules before a game is started. Crews working a park for the first time of a season should survey the park in ample time prior to a game to acquaint themselves of all physical peculiarities of the park. Do not hesitate to ask questions in the pre-game conference if you have any doubts.

7.10 NATIONAL ANTHEM

During the national anthem, all umpires are to stand at attention, heels together, head steady, facing the flag with cap in right hand placed over the heart, and left arm extended downward along the left pants leg. There is to be **no talking** during the national anthem.

If the crew remains together at home plate during the playing of the national anthem, they should stand in a straight line behind home plate facing the flag. Toes should be on the back line of the batters' boxes. It is permissible for the catcher to stand in line with the umpires.

If the crew members leave home plate before the playing of the national anthem, each umpire should be at attention when it is played.

7.11 PROPER POSITION BETWEEN INNINGS

The proper position for base umpires between innings is a few steps onto the outfield grass, approximately midway between first and second (or between second and third). Umpires should not stand in a position between innings which prompts conversation with players, managers, or coaches.

The proper position for the plate umpire between innings is on the first or third base foul line, one-fourth to one-half the way up the line from home plate.

The idea in each of these positions is for the umpire to be in a "neutral" position between innings, one which does not prompt conversations or confrontations with players, coaches, or managers.

If the plate umpire is having trouble during a particular inning, he is to go to the **opposite** foul line from that team's dugout between innings. The same holds true for base umpires. That is, if trouble can be expected from a player coming onto the field to take his position between innings, the base umpire should not station himself in an area which prompts a confrontation with that player.

7.12 LOCATION OF GROUNDSKEEPER

Always check with the groundskeeper to determine where he will be located in the event it is necessary to bring out the ground crew to cover the field or to turn on the lights.

7.13 OFFICIAL WATCH

When a game is to be played under a curfew or time limit or when inclement weather is forecast, one umpire on the crew should carry a watch, and his watch shall be considered official.

7.14 PROFANITY

Profanity that is audible to fans in the stands will not be tolerated. Umpires should not use profanity on the field; they are subject to the same disciplinary action as players. Umpires should never use any language on a player or manager which would result in disciplinary action if used on the umpire.

7.15 FRATERNIZATION

Umpires must not carry on idle conversations with coaches or players during the progress of a game or with other umpires unless proper officiating of the game requires it.

7.16 AFTER A BALL GAME

If the umpire-in-chief returns his unused supply of baseballs to the ball attendant, he should give them directly to the attendant or drop them directly into the game bag. He is not to toss them across the field to the attendant or toward the game bag.

At the conclusion of a game, umpires should refrain from congratulating fellow umpires while still on the field.

7.17 DRESS CODE

Remember that while both on and off the field, you are official representatives of Baseball. Dress accordingly to and from the ball park and when in public places. Always dress in a manner becoming to your position. Jeans and tennis shoes are not appropriate dress to and from the ball park.

7.18 TOBACCO

Use of chewing tobacco products is not permitted on the playing field for National Association umpires. (See Section 7.28, "Tobacco Ban Policy.")

7.19 MUSTACHES; HAIRCUTS

All National Association umpires are to be well groomed. Hair style and length should be in a manner consistent with your profession.

7.20 UNIFORMS; EQUIPMENT

All umpires on the crew are to be dressed in like manner except that the plate umpire has the option of wearing a shirt or plate coat; and the base umpire(s) have the option of wearing a shirt, sweater and shirt, rain (nylon) jacket, or uniform coat. The plate umpire may not wear a rain (nylon) jacket over his protector when working the plate. *Once in uniform, no umpire is to appear in public areas of the ball park other than under extenuating circumstances.*

Umpires are to keep their uniforms in good condition. Shoes should be polished, shirts and pants should be clean and pressed, and caps should be in good condition.

Class AAA umpires who are called up to the Major Leagues during the season are *not* to wear their Major League shirts or caps when returning to their minor league assignment.

It is mandatory in all National Association leagues that the plate umpire use an indicator during the game. Also, it is advisable that one of the umpires carry a watch each game (preferably *not* on his wrist) in case of possible rain situations or curfews.

7.21 SUNGLASSES

National Association umpires may not use sunglasses while on the field unless:

(1) A medical condition so requires, in which case a medical doctor's certification must be submitted beforehand to the league president or to the Executive Director of U.D.P.; or

(2) A special circumstance exists, in which case the situation must be approved beforehand by the league president or the Executive Director of U.D.P.

This regulation applies to regular and post-season games as well as to spring training and all post-season leagues.

7.22 RULE BOOK

Good umpiring means a complete knowledge of the rules, the application of a good common sense, and an ever-constant review of the Official Baseball Rules. You should read some portion of the rule book each day.

7.23 ATTITUDE

The following principles have been applied with success for many years and are considered sound. Incorporate them into your umpiring:

1. Cooperate with your partners. Help each other. Don't hesitate to ask for assistance if you are blocked out on a play. The main objective is to have all decisions ultimately correct.

2. Keep all personalities out of your work. You must be able to forgive and forget. Every game is a new game.

3. **Avoid sarcastic comments. Don't insist on the last word.** If, after an argument, a player is walking away—let him go!

4. Never charge a player or follow him if he is moving away; and do not point your finger or use violent gestures during an argument.

5. **Keep your temper.** A decision or an action taken in anger is never sound.

6. **Watch your language!** Never use language toward a player, coach, or manager which, if directed at the umpire, would result in the player, coach, or manager being disciplined.

7. If the manager has a legitimate point to argue under the rules, it is your duty to listen to him. An umpire can do this with dignity and no loss of respect. Be understanding—remember, the players are engaged in a heated contest. You are impartial judges and should **maintain a calm dignity** becoming the authority you have. **Be a good listener.**

8. Always keep your uniform in good condition.

9. Keep active and alert on the field at all times.

10. Keep the game moving. A ball game is often helped by energetic and earnest work of the umpires.

11. Be courteous, impartial, and firm, and so compel respect from all.

12. Remember that you are an official representative of Baseball both on and off the field. Act accordingly.

13. Always dress appropriately to and from the ball park and when in public places.

14. Even when off the field, remember that you continue to be representatives of Baseball and of your league. Never do anything that would bring disgrace upon your profession or upon Baseball. Always act, dress, and work in a way befitting your profession.

7.24 POSITIONING FOR PLAYS AT THE PLATE

The basic fundamental position for plays at the plate recommended by the Umpire Development Program for beginning professional umpires is the **first base line extended**. However, after gaining professional experience, it is permissible for veteran umpires to use alternative positions to take this play. In particular, following technique is acceptable for *experienced* umpires:

- Take the play by starting in the area between the first base line extended and the "point" of home plate, then swing to the **left** (i.e., first base line extended) or **right** (i.e., third base line extended), depending on the direction of the throw to the plate and the anticipated closeness of the play. In using this alternative, the plate umpire must be certain that he is completely set and not moving before the play occurs.

The alternative above takes into consideration the fact that if the play at the plate is a **swipe tag**, the optimal position is generally the ***third base line extended***; and if the play at the plate results in an actual **blocking of home plate**, the preferred position is the ***first base line extended***. Swipe tags often occur when the play is going to be close and the runner will attempt to elude the tag, while blocking of the plate can occur on a ground ball to the infield or on a play where the throw has the runner beat by a large margin. Also, swipe tags can occur when the catcher must reach out and take the throw from the *right side*, while blocking of the plate often occurs when the throw is coming from the catcher's *left side*. (These are simply guidelines, and if the umpire decides to implement an alternative position for plays at the plate, he must take each play independently and position himself accordingly.)

7.25 LEAGUE REGULATIONS

Each National Association league has a number of regulations/guidelines that are specific to that league. All umpires must be thoroughly familiar with these regulations, as these rules do vary from league to league. Do not fail to be in complete understanding of every one of your own league's regulations. A good opportunity to discuss these is at the individual league meeting prior to each season. As a starting list, make sure that you have answers to the following questions:

- Has the league adopted the optional suspended game rule? (See Section 5.7.)

- What is the league curfew (if any)? Are there certain periods during the season that the curfew is *not* in effect?

- How does the league president want you to inform him of ejections and other "trouble?"

- Does the league have an "equipment violation" policy (for example, regarding equipment thrown in disgust of an umpire's call)? If so, what is the league policy, and how is it to be enforced?

- Specifically when (if ever) are the umpires in charge of postponement responsibility prior to the start of a game? (See Section 5.11.)

- What is the lineup card format? Must a player be listed on the card in order to play?

- Is there a league limitation on the number of persons that may confer on the pitcher's mound at any one time?

- Does the league president have a preference or procedure as to how he wants the game balls to handled at the end of a game? Does he want them returned to the home club at the end of the game? Does he want the balls taken back to the umpires' room?

- Does the league have a policy on a "designated pitcher?" (That is, must a non-pitcher be listed specifically as a "designated pitcher" ("DP") on the lineup card in order for him to pitch in a game?)

- Does the league have any other specific regulations not mentioned elsewhere?

- What is the league's policy regarding game participation of traveling (roving) coaches and instructors? (See Section 1.26.)

- Does the home-team last-bat advantage transfer to the visiting city when a game is "transferred" and rescheduled as part of double-header in the opposing city?

7.26 RETENTION POLICY

The Baseball Office for Umpire Development will recommend to the minor leagues that a minor league umpire will be released if he/she is not hired by the next level league after completing the following maximum years in his/her current league:

1. A maximum of two years in the "Short A" leagues (rookie and other "short-season" leagues);

2. A maximum of two years in the "Long A" leagues (full-season leagues at the A level);

3. A maximum of two years at the AA level leagues; and

4. A maximum of four year at the AAA level leagues.

However, these time limits may be exceeded if one of the following occurs:

1. One of the major leagues expresses a clear interest that a particular umpire be retained based on that league's judgment that the umpire is still a viable candidate for selection to the major league level;

2. The umpire is invited to spring training with one of the major leagues; or

3. The umpire has been evaluated very favorably but has had limited exposure and evaluation by the next highest league.

In addition, the Baseball Office for Umpire Development may recommend for release, and/or any minor league may release, an umpire for any reason, including unsatisfactory performance or progress, before he/she would be recommended for release under this retention policy.

7.27 RATING CRITERIA; RATING SCALE

Umpires in all National Association leagues are evaluated by the Umpire Development Program in four categories, using a 1 through 5 scale, and employing the rating criteria on the following page.

7.28 TOBACCO BAN POLICY

Effective June 15, 1993, Major League Baseball and the National Association of Professional Baseball Leagues jointly instituted the following policy, which shall be strictly enforced and abided by all National Association umpires. (**Note:** Major League players on a rehab assignment with an N.A. club are *not* subject to the provisions of this policy.)

TOBACCO POLICY

For All National Association Leagues, Extended Spring Training, Instructional League, Hawaiian Winter League, and the Arizona Fall League

A) BAN AT THE BALLPARK AND DURING TEAM TRAVEL

The use or possession of tobacco (including, but not limited to, cigarettes, cigars, pipe tobacco, and smokeless tobacco) or any similar product (including, but not limited to, substitute products similar in appearance to tobacco) is prohibited, at all times, in all parts of the ballpark and during team travel. This includes, but is not limited to, the home and visitors' clubhouse, umpires' dressing room, bullpen, dugout, batting cages, and the grandstands during pre-game and post-game workouts, games, and all practices, and during all team travel, including bus, van, rail, or air transportation.

B) PERSONNEL COVERED BY THIS POLICY

All managers, coaches, instructors, trainers, players, umpires, field and clubhouse personnel, bat boys/girls and all visiting Major League administrative personnel.

C) RESPONSIBILITY FOR ENFORCEMENT OF POLICY

All violations of this policy are to be reported by the following personnel on the form provided by the Commissioner's Office:

MANAGERS

Managers shall be held responsible for eliminating the use and

PLATE

• Judgment of strike zone
• Consistency of strike zone
• Mechanics/style/form
• Use of voice
• Feet, body, head positioning
• Timing behind the plate
• Hustle/mobility/coordination
• Reactions to development of
  plays
• Communication with partner(s)
• General demeanor behind the
  plate
• Appearance

BASES

• Judgment of plays
• Positioning for plays
• Mechanics/style/form
• Use of voice
• Timing for plays
• Hustle/mobility/coordination
• Reactions to development of
  plays
• Communication with partner(s)
• General demeanor on the bases
• Appearance

CONSISTENCY OF ATTITUDE

• Focus on the game
• Game intensity/alertness
• Enthusiasm
• Projection of confidence
• Body language
• Fraternization
• Eagerness to learn and improve
• Willingness to accept construc-
  tive criticism
• Relationship with crew and
  others
• Professionalism on and off the
  field

HANDLING OF NON-ROUTINE SITUATIONS

• Knowledge/application of rules
  and interpretations
• Demeanor/poise during situations
• Overall ability in handling situations (verbal communication, taking action, tact, professionalism)
• Handling of pressure
• Overall projection of strength
  and professionalism during
  demanding situations on and off
  the field.

Below is the rating scale used by the Umpire Development Program when evaluating umpires in all National Association leagues:

5- OUTSTANDING — Virtually flawless and superior performance in this category.

4- ABOVE AVERAGE — A high standard of performance; above that of most umpires.

3- AVERAGE — Usual quality of work expected of an umpire at this level.

2- BELOW AVERAGE — Less than the usual quality expected in the league, yet at or above the minimum require-ments.

1- SUBSTANDARD — Below the minimum quality of work, not an acceptable rating for continuation at this level.

possession of tobacco or any similar product by coaches, instructors, trainers, players, field and clubhouse personnel, and bat boys/girls at the ballpark and during all team travel, and for reporting such violations to the Commissioner's Office.

UMPIRES

Umpires shall be held responsible for reporting/ejecting violators of this policy that occur on the playing field, in the bullpens and dugouts. If an umpire fails to report/eject personnel who are in violation of the policy, a report shall be filed in the umpire's evaluation record.

COMPLIANCE PERSONNEL

Compliance personnel representing the Commissioner's Office shall periodically check for violations in the ballpark, clubhouses and umpires' dressing room, during games and during team travel.

D) ELIMINATION OF TOBACCO SUPPLY

All managers and athletic trainers shall dispose of all tobacco or similar products that are available or in storage in the clubhouse, dugout or bullpen and all club personnel shall dispose of their own personal supply within the ballpark. No tobacco or similar products shall be stored in these areas, including free samples provided by various companies, or brought into the ballpark by players or any other club personnel.

E) PENALTIES FOR VIOLATIONS

The following penalties shall be imposed on the personnel shown below:

MANAGERS

Managers shall be ejected for any on-field violation of the ban by himself, a player, coach, instructor or trainer. In addition, a manager shall be fined by the Commissioner's Office according to the scale set forth below if he violates the ban, or knowingly permits violations by players, coaches, instructors or trainers and fails to report same.

COACHES, INSTRUCTORS, TRAINERS AND PLAYERS

Violations on the field, including dugout and bullpen:
All on-field violators including those in the dugout and bullpen shall be ejected from the game (including pre-game) immediately by the umpire. The manager shall be ejected at the same time if the violator is a coach, player, instructor or trainer. No warning shall be given. In addition, the Commissioner's Office

shall fine violators according to the scale set forth below.

Violations in the clubhouse or other parts of the ballpark, and during team travel:
Violators in the clubhouse or other parts of the ballpark or during team travel shall be fined by the Commissioner's Office according to the scale set forth below. The manager is responsible for reporting any violations.

UMPIRES
Umpires in violation of the tobacco policy shall be fined by the Commissioner's Office according to the scale set forth below.

BAT BOYS/GIRLS; FIELD AND CLUBHOUSE PERSONNEL
If a bat boy/girl or any other field or clubhouse personnel employed by the club violates the tobacco policy, he/she shall be instructed to leave the ballpark. A second violation shall result in dismissal from the club for the rest of the season.

F) SCHEDULE OF FINES
For each violation of this policy which calls for a fine, it shall be imposed in an amount as follows:

Single A, Short Season A, Rookie, Extended Spring Training, Hawaiian Winter League, and Instructional League personnel—$100;

Triple A, Double A, and Arizona Fall League personnel—$300.

7.29 ON-FIELD BEHAVIOR POLICY

In December of 1993, the On-Field Behavior Policy was established by the National Association of Professional Baseball Clubs in conjunction with Major League Baseball. For 1996 and 1997 the policy was modified slightly. The changes for those years involve some changes in penalties but do not change any enforcement guidelines as far as the umpires are concerned. The modifications to the policy for 1996 and 1997 include:

1. **Instigators and combatants** of the confrontations are "singled out" under the revised policy, and fines/suspensions have been increased for these personnel. The minimum fines for **instigators or combatants** are $450 at Triple-A; $300 at Double-A; $150 at Single-A Full Season; and $75 at Short-Season A and Rookie. The automatic minimum suspension for such violators is three games.

2. Players **leaving their positions** to involve themselves in a confrontation will be fined $150, $100, $50, and $25 respectively. How-

ever, such personnel are not subject to an automatic suspension.

3. The decision as to whether a player is deemed to have been an **instigator or combatant** in a confrontation is left to the discretion of the league president.

4. If a pitcher is judged by the league president to have intentionally thrown at a batter, an **automatic** fine and suspension applies (in addition to the pitcher's immediate ejection from the game).

Again, none of the above changes affect in any manner the way in which an umpire shall deal with or report on-field confrontations. The reports to the league president must be done with care and preciseness, and all umpires must be diligent and conscientious in their reporting.

The reports MUST be accurate and complete, and although difficult at times for the umpires, the report is expected to contain everything that occurred during the confrontation.

Note that Major League players on a rehab assignment with an N.A. club **are** *subject to the provisions of this policy and are to be reported in the same manner as any player.*

The actual text of the 1997 policy follows.

ON FIELD BEHAVIOR POLICY
For All National Association Leagues, Extended Spring Training, Instructional League, Hawaiian Winter League and the Arizona Fall League

Pitchers Intentionally Throwing at Hitters

A pitcher judged by the plate umpire to have intentionally delivered a pitched ball at a batter will be ejected from the game per Section 8.02(d)(1) of the Official Playing Rules.

At the time of the ejection the umpire shall warn the manager of both teams that another such pitch by any pitcher during the game will result in the immediate expulsion of the pitcher and that pitcher's manager.

Field Personnel Leaving Their Position to Participate in Confrontations

For purposes of this policy, applicable field personnel shall be defined as players/coaches/trainers/roving instructors.

The position of applicable field personnel is considered to be wherever the individual is located (dugout, bullpen, coaching box, defensive position, etc.) at the time a confrontational situation develops.

A player or players deemed by the League President to have been an instigator or combatant in a confrontation will receive an automatic fine (**minimum** $450 at Triple-A, $300 at Double-A, $150 at Single-A Full Season, $75 at Single-A Short Season and Rookie) and a **minimum** of a three game suspension. Such violations will include but not be limited to: a pitcher judged by the League President to have intentionally delivered a pitched ball at a batter, a pitcher leaving the pitcher's mound and initiating a confrontation, a batter/runner charging or pursuing the pitcher, fighting, etc.

A player involved in a confrontation while remaining at his position and judged to have been defending himself and not contributing to the incident will not be ejected, fined or suspended.

All applicable field personnel leaving their position to in any way involve themselves in a confrontation as other than an instigator or combatant will be fined by the League President based on the degree of their involvement.* **Minimum** fines for leaving their position will be $150 at Triple-A, $100 at Double-A, $50 at Single-A Full Season, $25 at Single-A Short Season and Rookie. The violator's conduct will be the basis for the League President's decision on whether a penalty greater than the minimum is appropriate.

If a violation of this policy does occur and a confrontation develops, the field managers/coaches/roving instructors are expected to leave their position as necessary, in an attempt to bring the violator(s) from their team under control. Staff should not involve themselves in physically restraining personnel from an opposing team.

Any player not currently on the active list (disabled or otherwise) leaving his position to become involved in a confrontation will be subject to the same penalties as an active player. Any suspension involving an inactive player will be served immediately upon activation.

* *Should a skirmish develop while other players are located nearby (i.e., a rundown, a play at second base involving the runner and the shortstop or second baseman with the other nearby, or a play at the plate involving the runner and catcher with the pitcher backing up), those "nearby" or "backing up" the play must not become involved as this will constitute a violation for leaving their position at the time a confrontational situation develops.*

NOTE: At no time will more than two position players and one pitcher concurrently serve suspensions. The length of suspension for pitchers will vary based on his position as a starting or relief pitcher. The League President will determine when suspensions will be served. All suspensions under this policy are to be without pay.

Notes:

a. In the case of Instructional League and Extended Spring Training all fines and suspensions shall be handled the same as the Rookie level and shall be determined by the Commissioner's Office.

b. In the case of the Arizona Fall League all fines and suspensions shall be handled the same as Triple-A and shall be determined by the Commissioner's Office.

b. In the case of the Arizona Fall League all fines and suspensions shall be handled the same as Triple-A and shall be determined by the Commissioner's Office.

c. In the case of the Hawaiian Winter League all fines and suspensions shall be handled the same as Single-A Full Season and shall be determined by the Commissioner's Office.

7.30 POLICY ON OPEN WOUNDS DURING GAME

In accordance with a directive from the Commissioner's Office dated March 17, 1993, all N.A. umpires shall abide by the M.L.B. policy regarding incidents in which a player begins bleeding during a game.

As the policy states, *"It is important for all umpires to know that some precautions will be taken that may cause brief delays in a game. For example, if a garment(s) is penetrated by blood or other potentially infectious materials, the garment(s) shall be removed immediately or as soon as feasible."*

Umpires are instructed to use good common sense in applying this directive. Excessive delays are not expected, but, in extreme cases the situation should be dealt with immediately. In most cases it is expected that the problem can be resolved between innings; however, there may be cases when the situation must be acted upon immediately.

SECTION 8

MECHANICS FOR THE THREE-UMPIRE SYSTEM

8.1 NO RUNNERS ON BASE

1. The first base umpire should be about 10-12 feet behind the first baseman with both feet in foul territory. The third base umpire should be in the same approximate position behind the third baseman.

2. If the third base umpire is required to go out to the outfield to render a decision, you will revert back to the two-umpire system. Anytime you go out, **don't try to get back into the play**; wait until all action has ceased before returning to your position.

3. If the first base umpire goes out, the third base umpire will come straight into the center of the infield and take any play at second or third base on the batter-runner. The plate umpire will come down to first base and be responsible for the batter-runner touching first base and will take any play on the batter-runner returning to first base. The plate umpire will not release the responsibility of batter-runner until the first base umpire has assumed his position after returning from the outfield. Should the batter-runner continue past first, second, and third, the play at the plate, if any, will be the responsibility of the plate umpire.

4. With no runners on base, the third base umpire will come straight across to second base on all ground balls and fly balls to the infield and take all plays at second base and third base. The first base umpire will come in and set up in a position needed to render a decision at first base.

5. With no runners on base, the third base umpire will come straight across the infield toward second base on all fly balls, line drives, and base hits to the outfield and render all decisions on the batter-runner going into second base unless, of course, he has found it necessary to go out to the outfield. The first base umpire will come into the infield on all fly balls and line drives to the left side of the outfield (from the center fielder straight in and to the center fielder's right) whether or not the third base umpire goes out. If the ball is not hit in the air to the left side of the outfield, the first base umpire

will drift toward the direction of first base so as to be in proper position for any play on the batter-runner returning to first base. (See item 7 below.)

6. With no runners on base, if the batter hits a base hit to the outfield which goes beyond or through the outfielder, the third base umpire will start toward second base, and the first base umpire will come in and pivot watching the batter-runner touch first and will continue to take the batter-runner into second. The third base umpire, seeing the ball has gone through the outfielder, will then hold up and be ready to take the batter-runner into third base. However, if the ball stays in front of the outfielder and is bobbled or is a slow hit ball and the batter-runner tries to stretch it into a double, the third base umpire—who has started across the infield—will be responsible for the play at second base. The first base umpire—who has come in and pivoted—will watch the batter-runner touch first and release the batter-runner to the third base umpire for the play at second base. Both **verbal and hand** signals should be used to communicate with each other during this situation. Remember that if there is a **play** on the batter-runner at second base in this situation, it belongs to the third base umpire. If there is **no play** at second base (i.e., the batter hits a stand-up double), the first base umpire should take the batter-runner into second. Also, in situations where the ball gets loose *after the play at second* and the batter-runner attempts to reach third base, the plate umpire will be responsible for the play at third, and the first base umpire will cover home if necessary.

7. On all fly balls where neither umpire goes out, if the fly ball is to left field, left center, or where the center fielder is coming straight in as the third base umpire is coming straight across the infield toward second base, the responsibility of the catch or no catch decision will belong to the third base umpire. The responsibility of the play at second also belongs to the third base umpire. *(The third base umpire should not "rim" along the edge of the outfield grass in order to cover these responsibilities.)* On fly balls hit to right center or right field where neither umpire has gone out, the responsibility of the catch or no catch and the touching of first base belongs to the first base umpire.

8.2 RUNNER ON FIRST BASE ONLY

1. The first base umpire will position himself 6-8 feet beyond the first base bag with both feet in foul territory for the pick-off play at first

base. You should be close enough to make the decision on a pick off without moving into the play.

2. The third base umpire will move into the center of the infield and assume a position on either side of second base that is most comfortable for him to take the steal play at second base. (Normally you will set up on the side of second base opposite the pitching arm. However, it is left up to you as to which side you are most comfortable in taking the steal play.) You will never be on the outfield side of the bag-always on the inside of the infield.

3. If the runner on first is picked off, the infield umpire will have that part of the rundown going into second base and any subsequent play into third base. The first base umpire should move toward second base as the runner continues on to third base and assume responsibility for the back end of a possible rundown between second and third base. The first base umpire should not commit toward second until after the runner has gained possession of second base since the runner over rounding second and returning is the responsibility of the third base umpire.

4. With a runner on first base only, if the first base umpire goes out for any reason, the infield umpire should slide over toward first base and assume full responsibility for the runner on first base and also have responsibility should the batter become a runner. The plate umpire should go down to third base and take the play on the runner coming from first base, and if that runner continues on to home plate, the plate umpire will also have that responsibility. *In this situation it is also permissible for the plate umpire to move up the first base line to take any play at first base on the runner returning after a fly ball or line drive is caught.*

5. With a runner on first base only, if the first base umpire does not go out to the outfield, then on a base hit, after the batter-runner touches first base, the first base umpire will start to move in the direction of home. The infield umpire, after watching the runner on first touch second and seeing that he has **committed** to third, will assume responsibility for the batter-runner going to second or returning to first base. The plate umpire will move in the direction of third base and will go into the cutout if there is any likelihood that the runner from first will advance to third on the batted ball. If it is obvious that the runner will not advance to third, it is not necessary for the plate umpire to go all the way to third. If the plate umpire does move into the cutout, he will remain at third base

until all action has ceased. After the first base umpire has watched the batter-runner touch first and has seen the runner on first **committed** to third base, he will come to the plate for any play on the runner from first base coming to the plate. However, if the runner originally on first does not go to third base, the first base umpire cannot over-commit to the plate and will have the responsibility for the batter-runner returning to first base. As the first base umpire, do not commit to home until the runner from first has committed to third.

6. With a runner on first base only, if the infield umpire goes out for any reason, you will revert back to the two-umpire system.

7. With a runner on first base only, the responsibility of catch or no catch of fly balls and line drives to the outfield belongs to the infield umpire. If the ball is hit down the right field foul line or if the ball is hit where the right fielder comes straight in, then the catch/no catch responsibility belongs to the first base umpire. If the ball is hit where the left fielder moves any distance toward the foul line, then the catch/no catch responsibility belongs to the plate umpire.

(Note that some crews prefer to have the first base umpire cover all fly balls and line drives from the center fielder straight in all the way to the right field line. The infield umpire would then take the center fielder moving to his right all the way to the left fielder moving straight in. The plate umpire would take the left fielder moving to his right. These are also acceptable mechanics for fly ball/line drive coverage with a runner on first base only.)

8.3 RUNNERS ON FIRST AND SECOND; LESS THAN TWO OUT

1. The first base umpire will position himself 6-8 feet behind the first baseman with both feet in foul territory.

2. The third base umpire will position himself halfway between the pitcher's mound and second base on the third base side of the mound in a position ready for plays at second or third.

3. With runners on first and second base, fly ball and line drive responsibility remains the same as with a runner on first base only. The plate umpire will remain home. The tag up at second base and the possible play at third belongs to the infield umpire. The tag up at first belongs to the first base umpire, but the play at second base belongs to the infield umpire. Again, let the ball take you to your play.

An optional method of covering the tag up with runners on first and second is for the plate umpire to take the play at third on the runner tagging up at second. In this case, the third base umpire will slide over and take responsibility of the runner on first base, and the first base umpire will move home to cover a possible play at the plate. This would be a crew mechanic and should be clearly understood by each member of the crew.

4. With runners on first and second base, on any base hit the plate umpire will remain at **home**, and the first and third base umpires will assume responsibility for all plays on the bases. On a base hit, the first base umpire will pivot and take the batter-runner into second; he is responsible for any play made on the batter-runner at second base or back into first base.

5. With runners on first and second base, if the infield umpire goes out on a fly ball, the plate umpire will move up toward third base and the first base umpire will come into the center of the infield. If both runners are tagging up to advance, both tag-up responsibilities belong to the first base umpire, and the play at third base on the runner from second base belongs to the plate umpire. The play at second base on the runner from first base and the responsibility of the runner from first belong to the first base umpire.

6. With runners on first and second base, if the first base umpire goes out, you will revert back to the two-umpire system.

7. With runners on first and second base and an obvious bunting situation, the third base umpire will stay behind third, and the first base umpire will move into the center of the infield setting up on the first base side of the infield. This is optional; however, it is much easier to cover the force play at third should the defense decide to throw there.

8.4 RUNNERS ON FIRST AND SECOND; TWO OUT

1. The third base umpire will position himself 6-8 feet behind the third baseman.

2. The first base umpire will position himself halfway between the pitcher's mound and second base on the first base side of the mound.

3. With runners on first and second with two out, fly ball and line drive responsibilities remain the same as with runners on second and third. The plate umpire will remain at home.

4. With runners on first and second with two out, on any ball hit, the third base umpire is responsible for the touching of third base and possible plays at third base. The infield umpire is responsible for the touching of first and second and possible plays at first and second base, including plays on the batter-runner.

5. Note that some crews prefer to leave the first base umpire at first base with runners on first and second with two out. This is permissible, and in that case the mechanics for fly balls and base hits would be the same as in Section 8.3 of this manual.

8.5   BASES LOADED; LESS THAN TWO OUT

1. The first base umpire will position himself 6-8 feet behind the first baseman with both feet in foul territory.

2. The third base umpire will position himself halfway between the pitcher's mound and second base on the third base side of the mound in a position ready for plays at second or third.

3. On balls hit to the infield, the infield umpire will render all decisions at second and third base. The first base umpire will render all decisions at first base. The plate umpire will remain at the plate.

4. On fly balls and line drives to the outfield where neither umpire goes out, the infield umpire will be responsible for the catch/no catch on all balls hit directly at the left fielder and between the left fielder and the right fielder moving toward center field. The first base umpire will be responsible for fly balls directly at the right fielder. *(See Section 8.2, Item 7 for alternate catch/no catch responsibilities.)*

5. If the infield umpire goes out for any reason, the first base umpire will come into the center of the infield, and you will revert back to the two-umpire system. If the first base umpire goes out for any reason, you will again revert back to the two-umpire system for all coverages.

6. The tagging up by the runner on third base belongs to the home plate umpire. The tagging up by the runner on second base going to third belongs to the infield umpire. The tagging up by the runner on first base going to second belongs to the first base umpire. Remember to let the ball take you to your play.

7. With bases loaded and less than two out, on any base hit the plate umpire will remain at **home**, and the first and third base umpires will assume responsibility for all plays on the bases. On a base hit,

the first base umpire will pivot and take the batter-runner into second; he is responsible for any play made on the batter-runner at second base or back into first base.

8.6   BASES LOADED; TWO OUT

1. The third base umpire will position himself 6-8 feet behind the third baseman.

2. The first base umpire will position himself halfway between the pitcher's mound and second base on the first base side of the pitcher's mound.

3. With bases loaded and two out, fly ball and line drive responsibilities remain the same as with runners on second and third. The plate umpire will remain home.

4. With bases loaded and two out, on any ball hit, the third base umpire is responsible for the touching of third base and possible plays at third base. The infield umpire is responsible for the touching of first and second base and possible plays at first and second base, including plays on the batter-runner.

5. Note that some crews prefer to leave the first base umpire at first base with bases loaded and two out. This is permissible, and in that case the mechanics for fly balls and base hits would be the same as in Section 8.5 of this manual.

8.7   RUNNERS ON FIRST AND THIRD; LESS THAN TWO OUT

1. The third base umpire will position himself halfway between the pitcher's mound and second base on the third base side of the mound in a position ready for plays at second or third.

2. The first base umpire will position himself 6-8 feet beyond the first base bag with both feet in foul territory.

3. Fly ball responsibility remains the same as with runners on first and second or with a runner on first base only. The plate umpire is responsible for the runner on third tagging up and advancing to home plate.

4. With runners on first and third base and less than two out, on a base hit the plate umpire will come up to third base and assume the responsibility of the runner going to third base from first base. The infield umpire, after watching the runner from first base touch second base and seeing that he is in fact going to advance to third base,

will slide over to the first base side of the mound and assume responsibility for the batter-runner advancing to second base or returning to first base. After the first base umpire has watched the batter-runner touch first and has seen the runner on first **committed** to third base, he will come to the plate for any possible play there.

5. With runners on first and third base and less than two out, on a fly ball where the runner on third is tagging up, the responsibility for the tag up and the play at the plate belongs to the plate umpire. The first base umpire will come in and pivot, lining up the tag from first base and assuming responsibility of the runner on first. The infield umpire has the responsibility for the play at second base. Should the runner tagging up at third base hold up and return to third base, the infield umpire also has responsibility for the play back into third. In that situation (play back into third), if the runner on first base tags up and goes into second base, the responsibility for him belongs to the first base umpire.

8.8 RUNNERS ON FIRST AND THIRD; TWO OUT

1. The third base umpire will position himself 6-8 feet behind the third baseman with both feet in foul territory.

2. The first base umpire will position himself halfway between the pitcher's mound and second base on the first base side of the mound.

3. With runners on first and third base with two out, on any ball hit, the plate umpire shall remain at home plate for possible plays. The third base umpire remains at third base for the touching of third and possible plays at that base. The infield umpire is responsible for plays at first and second, including plays on the batter-runner.

4. With runners on first and third with two out, fly ball and line drive responsibilities remain the same as with runners on second and third. The plate umpire will remain at home.

5. Note that some crews prefer to leave the first base umpire at first base with runners on first and third and two out. This is permissible, and in that case the mechanics for fly balls and base hits would be the same as in Section 8.7 of this manual.

8.9 RUNNER ON SECOND BASE ONLY

1. With a runner on second base only, the third base umpire will position himself 6-8 feet behind the third baseman with both feet in foul territory.

2. The first base umpire will position himself in the infield setting up on the first base side of the infield on the edge of infield grass, approximately 10-12 feet from second base.

3. On any ball hit to an infielder, the third base umpire will be responsible for all plays at third base. The infield umpire will be responsible for all plays at second and first.

4. On fly balls and line drives to the outfield, the responsibility for the catch or no catch belongs to the infield umpire **unless** the ball is hit down the third base line or to the left fielder coming straight in or going to the foul line. In that case, the responsibility will belong to the third base umpire, who is on the foul line. With an umpire on the third base line and one in the center of the infield, on any ball hit where the right fielder moves any distance toward the foul line, the responsibility for fair/foul and catch/no catch belongs to the home plate umpire.

(Note that with a runner on second base only, some crews prefer to have the third base umpire take responsibility for coverage from the center fielder straight in all the way to the left field line. In this situation the first base umpire would take the center fielder moving to his left all the way to the right fielder coming straight in. The plate umpire would then take the right fielder moving toward his left. These are also acceptable mechanics.)

5. With a runner on second base only, if the infield umpire goes out, the third base umpire will come into the center of the infield, and you will revert back to the two-umpire system.

6. If the third base umpire goes out for any reason, you will again revert back to the two-umpire system.

8.10 RUNNERS ON SECOND AND THIRD

1. With runners on second and third base, the third base umpire will position himself 6-8 feet behind the third baseman with both feet in foul territory.

2. The first base umpire will position himself in the infield setting up on the first base side of the infield on the edge of the infield grass, approximately 10-12 feet from second base.

3. On any ball hit to an infielder, the third base umpire will be responsible for all plays at third base. The infield umpire will be responsible for all plays at first and second.

4. On fly balls and line drives to the outfield, the responsibility for the catch or no catch belongs to the infield umpire **unless** the ball is hit down the third base line or to the left fielder coming straight in or going to the foul line. In those cases, the responsibility will belong to the third base umpire, who is on the foul line. With an umpire on the third base line and one in the center of the infield, on any ball hit where the right fielder moves any distance toward the foul line, the responsibility for fair/foul and catch/no catch belongs to the home plate umpire. *(See Section 8.9, Item 4 for optional method of covering fly balls and line drives to the outfield with runners on second and third.)*

5. With runners on second and third base, if the infield umpire goes out, the third base umpire will come into the center of the infield, and you will revert back to the two-umpire system.

6. With runners on second and third base, if the third base umpire goes out for any reason, you will again revert back to the two-umpire system.

8.11 RUNNER ON THIRD BASE ONLY

1. With a runner on third base only, the third base umpire will position himself 6-8 feet behind the third baseman with both feet in foul territory.

2. The first base umpire will position himself 10-12 feet behind the first baseman with both feet in foul territory.

3. On balls hit to the infield, the third base umpire will remain at third base for a possible play there. The first base umpire will come in and set up for a possible play at first base. Should the ball be overthrown, then the first base umpire will continue on into the infield, pivot, and take the batter-runner into second base or back into first base.

4. On a fly ball where the runner from third base may be tagging up to advance, the third base umpire will position himself in such a position as to line up the tag. The first base umpire will come in and pivot, assuming full responsibility for the batter-runner going into second base or returning to first base should the ball be dropped.

5. On a clean base hit, the third base umpire will come into the infield and take responsibility for the batter-runner going into second base **except** that the responsibility for the batter-runner on a stand-up double will be the same as outlined in paragraph 6 of Section 8.1,

"No Runners on Base." The first base umpire will come in, pivot, and take the batter-runner into second base or back into first base, again as outlined in paragraph 6 of Section 8.1 of this manual.

6. With a runner on third base only, if the third base umpire goes out, the first base umpire will come in, pivot, and take responsibility for the batter-runner. You will then revert back to the two-umpire system.

7. With a runner on third base only, if the first base umpire goes out, the third base umpire will come into the center of the infield and take responsibility for the batter-runner going into second base or returning to first base. The home plate umpire will drop back into foul territory and take responsibility for the runner on third tagging up. In this situation, the third base umpire is responsible for the batter-runner touching first base.

8. With a runner on third base only, on a fly ball or line drive from left field to center field where neither umpire goes out, the third base umpire will have responsibility of the tag up at third base and will also have the responsibility of the catch/no catch decisions. The first base umpire will come in, pivot, and take responsibility of the batter-runner going into second base or returning to first base.

8.12 CHECKED SWINGS

When the batter checks his swing and the plate umpire requests help from his partner, the plate umpire shall, in all cases, ask the first base umpire with a right-handed batter at bat or the third base umpire with a left-handed batter at bat.

SECTION 9

MECHANICS FOR THE FOUR-UMPIRE SYSTEM

9.1 GENERAL PRINCIPLES

One of the key concepts in understanding four-umpire mechanics concerns the position of the second base umpire and the coverage of fly balls/line drives to the outfield when runners are on base. If the crew is working "American League style," one umpire goes out on **every** fly ball or line drive to the outfield, no matter how routine or how difficult and no matter how many outs or who is on base. If the crew is working "National League style," an umpire goes out only when the play is going to be **difficult** (for example, a shoestring catch, home run, ball off the outfield wall, three fielders converging on the ball, a catch made at the wall or warning track, etc.).

Whenever runners are on first only, second only, first and second, first and third, second and third, or bases loaded the second base umpire will position himself on the **inside** of second base (with the **exceptions** covered in Sections 9.5 and 9.9). With no runners on base or a runner on third base only, the second base umpire will position himself behind second base. The basic idea here is that whenever a steal or double play is in order, the second base umpire is to be on the inside at second base (again, with the exceptions permissible in Sections 9.5 and 9.9).

Another important concept to remember is that *whenever one umpire goes out, the crew will revert to a three-umpire system.* (Refer to Section 8 for basic mechanics of the three-umpire system.)

9.2 NO RUNNERS ON BASE

With no runners on base the second base umpire will position himself behind second base, several feet onto the outfield grass. He may position himself shaded toward the first base or third base side behind second base, although normally he will position himself on the "pull" side of the hitter.

The second base umpire has responsibility for all fly balls and line drives to the outfield *except* those hit down the foul lines requiring a fair/foul ruling. (**Note:** With no runners on base, some less experienced crews may prefer to have the second base umpire cover fly balls and line drives from the left fielder *straight in* (or straight back) all the way to the right fielder *straight in* (or straight back). Using this method, the first base umpire would then be responsible for all balls to the outfield where the right fielder moves any distance to his *left*, and the third base umpire would take all balls to the outfield where the left fielder moves any distance to his *right*. Either of the two methods described in this paragraph are acceptable.)

If the crew is working American League style, an umpire would go out on every fly ball or line drive to the outfield. If the crew is working National League style, the umpire would go out only if he anticipates a difficult play in the outfield (using the "pause-read-react" technique described in the *Manual for the Two-Umpire System*). However, if an umpire uses the National League style and chooses not to go out on a fly ball, he must realize that he still has responsibility for the catch/no catch.

Remember that if one umpire goes out in this situation, the crew will revert back to a three-umpire system.

9.3 RUNNER ON FIRST BASE ONLY

With a runner on first base only, the second base umpire will position himself on the inside at second base. He may position himself on either the shortstop or first base side of the bag—whichever side he is more comfortable working. A general rule of thumb is for the umpire to position himself on the opposite side of the pitcher's throwing arm (i.e., on the shortstop side for left-handed pitchers and on the second base side for right-handed pitchers). However, this is not a requirement, and the umpire may position himself on whichever side he prefers. He should set up with his feet on the edge of the infield grass a few feet down from the edge of the cutout at second base. He may set up with his feet parallel to grass line OR he may square himself with home plate. Either method is acceptable.

See Section 9.4 regarding coverage of balls hit to the outfield in this situation.

If the first base umpire goes out with a runner on first base only with less than two out, the plate umpire will cover at first base. If the third base umpire goes out, the crew will rotate (although with two out some crews prefer *not* to rotate and instead let the second base umpire slide over to third). If the second base umpire goes out, the crew would revert to a three-umpire system (i.e., depending on the play the crew would either rotate or the first base umpire would come into the middle of the infield).

9.4 COVERING BALLS TO THE OUTFIELD WHEN SECOND BASE UMPIRE IS POSITIONED INSIDE

As mentioned in Section 9.1, if the crew is working American League style, one umpire *must* go out on every fly ball or line drive to the outfield; if working the National League style, an umpire goes out only when the play appears to be difficult. *The crew **must** predetermine which method they will use.*

In addition to the above two alternatives, there are two other options as to coverage when the second base umpire is positioned *inside* the infield. Specifically, either one of the following methods of covering fly balls to the outfield is acceptable when the second base umpire is inside:

1. The *wing umpires* (i.e., the first and third base umpires) take *all* balls to the outfield. If a crew chooses to use this method, the third base umpire takes from the center fielder *straight in* (or straight back) all the way to the left field line. The first base umpire would then take everything from the center fielder moving any distance to his *left* all the way to the right field line; OR

2. The second base umpire *goes out from the inside*. In using this alternative, the second base umpire would take everything from the left fielder moving any distance to his left all the way to the right fielder moving any distance to his right. The first and third base umpires would then take any balls from the right and left fielders *straight in* (or straight back) respectively all the way to the foul lines.

Either of the above two methods are acceptable. Each has its strong points and drawbacks, and neither one is preferred over the other. The important thing is that the crew is *certain* which method they are using (as well as whether they are using American or National League style of covering fly balls). These facts must be clearly predetermined by the crew.

9.5 RUNNER ON SECOND BASE ONLY

With a runner on second base only, the second base umpire will position himself on the *inside* at second base as described in Section 9.3. However, there is an "exception" to this positioning—namely, with a runner on second base only, it is also permissible for the second base umpire to position himself behind the second base bag (on the dirt of the infield on the third base side only).

If the second base umpire positions himself on the **outside** of the bag, fly ball coverage would be the same as with no runners on base. (NOTE: With less than two out, some crews prefer to modify this coverage slightly (having the first base umpire take from the center fielder to the foul line) in order to keep the second base umpire at second for the tag-up.) If the second base umpire goes out, the first base umpire must hustle in quickly to cover any plays at second base (as well as watch the tag-up at second). The first base umpire is also responsible for all plays at first base.

If the second base umpire stays on the **inside**, fly ball coverage would be the same as with a runner on first base (i.e., optional whether the second base umpire or the wing umpires go out). If the second base umpire goes out, the first base umpire must hustle into the middle to take any play at second (or at first). If the first or third base umpire goes out, the second base umpire would either slide over to cover possible plays depending on which wing umpire went out; OR the crew would *rotate*. Which method is used here depends on which way the crew has predetermined they will cover the situation. Either method is acceptable.

9.6   RUNNER ON THIRD BASE ONLY

With a runner on third base only, the second base umpire will position himself behind second base. He will not position himself as deeply in the outfield as with no runners on base since he may be required to slide over to cover plays at first or third base should one of the wing umpires go out. Fly ball and line drive coverage would be the same as with no runners on base. If the third base umpire goes out, the second base umpire would either slide over for any potential play back into third OR the crew would *rotate*, whichever they have predetermined. The plate umpire takes the tag-up at third base if the third base umpire goes out. If the first base umpire goes out, the second base umpire would slide over to take any play at first or second.

9.7   RUNNERS ON FIRST AND SECOND

With runners on first and second, the second base umpire would position himself on the inside of second base. Either side of second is permissible, although the general rule of thumb is to position on the opposite side of the throwing hand of the pitcher. However, the umpire may position himself on either side—whichever he is more comfortable working. Fly balls and line drives to the outfield are covered using the techniques described in Section 9.4 (i.e., either the second base umpire goes out from the middle OR the wing umpires go out—and the crew must predetermine which method they are using).

If the second base umpire goes out, the first base umpire must hustle in to the middle of the infield to take any play at second base (as well as watch the tag-up at second). The first base umpire is also responsible for all plays at first base.

If either the first or third base umpire goes out, the second base umpire would slide over to cover any plays at those bases, OR the crew would rotate, whichever way the crew predetermines they will use.

9.8   RUNNERS ON FIRST AND THIRD

With runners on first and second, the second base umpire would position himself on the inside of second base. Either side of second is permissible, although the general rule of thumb is to position on the opposite side of the throwing hand of the pitcher. However, the umpire may position himself on either side—whichever he is more comfortable working.

Fly ball and line drive coverage would be the same as described in Section 9.4 (i.e., either the second base umpire goes out from the middle OR the wing umpires go out). If the first base umpire goes out, the second base umpire must slide over to take any plays at first or second. If the third base umpire goes out, the second base umpire would either slide over and cover at third base OR the crew would rotate, whichever the crew has predetermined.

9.9   RUNNERS ON SECOND AND THIRD

With a runners on second and third, the second base umpire will position himself on the *inside* at second base as described in Section 9.3. However, there is an "exception" to this positioning—namely, with runners on second and third, it is also permissible for the second base umpire to position himself behind the second base bag (on the dirt of the infield on the third base side only).

If the second base umpire positions himself on the **outside** of the bag, fly ball coverage would be the same as with no runners on base. If the second base umpire goes out, the first base umpire must hustle in quickly to cover any plays at second base (as well as watch the tag-up at second). The first base umpire is also responsible for all plays at first base.

If the second base umpire stays on the **inside**, fly ball coverage would be the same as with a runner on first base (i.e., optional whether the second base umpire or the wing umpires go out). If the second base umpire goes out, the first base umpire must hustle into the middle to take any play at second (or at first); he would also have the tag-up at second base.

If the first or third base umpire goes out, the second base umpire would either slide over to cover possible plays depending on which wing umpire went out; OR the crew would *rotate*. Which method is used here depends on which way the crew has predetermined they will cover the situation. Either method is acceptable.

9.10   BASES LOADED

With bases loaded, the second base umpire would position himself on the inside of second base. Either side of second is permissible, although the general rule of thumb is to position on the opposite side of the throwing hand of the pitcher. However, the umpire may position himself on either side—whichever he is more comfortable working. Fly balls and line drives to the outfield are covered using the techniques described in Section 9.4 (i.e., either the second base umpire goes out from the middle OR the wing umpires go out-the crew must predetermine which method they are using).

If the second base umpire goes out, the first base umpire must hustle in to the middle of the infield to take any play at second base (as well as watch the tag-up at second). The first base umpire is also responsible for all plays at first base.

If either the first or third base umpire goes out, the second base umpire would slide over to cover any plays at those bases, OR the crew would rotate-whichever method the crew predetermines they will use.